ONE FOR THE ROAD

ONE FOR THE ROAD

New Plays for One Actor

edited by Kit Brennan

EDITIONS

Cover design by Doowah Design.
This book was printed on Ancient Forest Friendly paper.
Printed and bound in Canada by Hignell Book Printing.

We acknowledge the support of the Canada Council for the Arts and the Manitoba Arts Council for our publishing program.

Library and Archives Canada Cataloguing in Publication

One for the road : new plays for one actor / Kit Brennan, editor.

ISBN 978-1-897109-96-0

1. Monologues, Canadian (English) — 21st century. 2. Canadian drama (English) — 21st century. I. Brennan, Kit, 1957-

PS8307 O54 2012   C812'.0450806   C2012-906326-6

Signature Editions
P.O. Box 206, RPO Corydon, Winnipeg, Manitoba, R3M 3S7
www.signature-editions.com

Contents

Information on Producing

To obtain permission for professional and amateur productions of any of the plays in this volume, contact the publisher:

Signature Editions
P.O. Box 206, RPO Corydon, Winnipeg, MB R3M 3S7
www.signature-editions.com
signature@allstream.net

or:

NGGRFG, Berend McKenzie, contact through Signature Editions

Cassandra, Briana Brown, contact through the Playwrights Guild of Canada

Dianne & Me, Ron Fromstein, ron.fromstein@gmail.com

All My Day Jobs, Kirsten Van Ritzen, broadtheatrics@yahoo.ca

Dear Penthouse, Collin Doyle, contact through the Playwrights Guild of Canada

Sunnyside Café, Pam Calabrese MacLean, contact through Signature Editions

Foreword

Plays for one actor are all about storytelling. As audience member, you become intrigued with the character on stage. Over the course of the evening, this character may play several or even many different characters while telling his or her story, but this world of people and events still appears before you in the body of one actor.

For this anthology, I read approximately sixty plays, and difficult decisions had to be made by the time I decided on a short list. Finally, I let the aspect of storytelling guide me. In its simplest form, storytelling is a low-tech art form. You have a teller, and an audience, and a story, and in the space where those three things connect, curiosity and enchantment grow. The teller shares a vision, the audience joins in and enhances that vision through their own imaginations, and the story takes everyone on a journey or a quest. It's continuous and doesn't let up until the story concludes and the teller drops you back onto the earth in a slightly different place than you were before. Even with all of the theatrical bells and whistles of design, light, sound and costumes, a play for one actor is still (mostly) about story.

These six plays are about characters looking into their pasts — literally stepping back into them, in many cases — in order to create (or recreate) a better present. Looking to their families for answers, or forgiveness, or for the strength to let go—or looking at themselves to get up and get out there, to change for the better. Some of them manage it, and some don't. A strong sense of humour enlivens many of these plays; a number of them also reveal deep sadness. Important issues are explored: sexuality, inter-racial adoption, teenage pregnancy, unemployment. Two are focused on mothers and daughters; one deals poignantly with a father and son. One play features a young girl almost too smart for her own good, wrestling with parents; another is of a young woman wrestling with jobs; and one is of a man wrestling with a fantasy that clashes with reality.

The writers come from all across Canada: Victoria, Vancouver, Edmonton, Toronto, and Antigonish. As suits the title of the collection, the scripts have been road-tested on stages large and small in almost every province, and in some cases, the playwrights are also the performers. Berend McKenzie's *Nggrfg* has been produced at Young People's Theatre in Toronto, and he has just returned from a successful run at the Edinburgh Fringe Festival. Briana Brown has performed *Cassandra* at fringe festivals in London, Ottawa, Victoria and Vancouver; Ron Fromstein's *Dianne & Me* has won three playwriting competitions, and been seen in Vancouver, Stratford, Toronto, and Hamilton. Kirsten van Ritzen has performed *All My Day Jobs* in Victoria, Regina and Vancouver; Collin Doyle performed *Dear Penthouse* at the Edmonton Fringe, and Pam McLean's *Sunnyside Café* has had a main stage production at Ship's Company Theatre in Parrsboro, Nova Scotia, and also played in Halifax and Goose Bay.

This collection is designed for those seeking new voices and new work for a solo actor. Should you wish to produce any of these plays, please remember that they are fully protected by copyright; see page 6, Information on Producing. The individual playwrights can be contacted through the particular addresses found on that page. I hope you enjoy the work!

I'd like to thank my partner, Andrew Willmer, for his stalwart assistance with this collection. A big thank you, too, to Samantha Beiko at Signature Editions, for keeping it all moving ahead smoothly.

— Kit Brennan,
Theatre Department, Concordia University,
Montreal, Quebec

Nggrfg
(Would you say the name of this play?)

by Berend McKenzie

Characters

BUDDY— various ages

Production History

NGGRFG (Would you say the name of this play?) first premiered at the 2009 Edmonton and Vancouver International Fringe Festivals. That same year, it ran at the Fire Hall Arts Centre, where it garnered a Jessie Award nomination for Outstanding Original Script. In 2009-2010, the Vancouver School Board produced a high school tour of the piece and commissioned an edited version of the last story, Tassels, to be performed in local elementary schools. *NGGRFG* was produced twice in Halifax: once at the Queer Acts Theatre Festival, and once at the Eastern Front Theatre's Super Nova Festival. In 2011, *NGGRFG* was produced at Toronto's Young People's Theatre. In 2012, *NGGRFG* made its European premiere at the Edinburgh Festival Fringe.

Liner — Age 16

Buddy: She said yes. I can't believe she said yes.

The air escapes the room every time Melanie McDougal enters it. She gives me hope, an excuse to get up in the morning and a reason to live.

I love the way she smells. She's so edgy and cool. No one in the school has hair like hers, a vicious Mohawk, and my favourite part, black eyeliner smudged underneath her eyes, which makes them real, intense. If I was a girl, I would wear my makeup just like Melanie's.

I have decided that she is the one. With her on my arm, school won't be such a terrifying place. With Melanie as my girlfriend, my street cred would go up significantly. When Melanie is finally mine, they won't call me fag anymore.

All I have to do is get rid of her jock boyfriend. Dozer. He's a six-foot-tall, 250-pound defensive tackle on the school football team. What a tool. Just the sound of his name gives me hives and kicks my asthma into high gear. I hate Dozer, only because he has what I so desperately need, Melanie McDougal.

Today she entered the classroom. Her head hung low. She dragged her feet along the floor. She took her seat.

Looks like Dozer's been using his human punching bag again.

I write Melanie a note.

"How are things between you and Dozer?"

How do you think?

"Are you guys going to the final bush party together?"

He's going with Stephanie Wilcox.

"You know she's a human Posture-Pedic?"

Oh, Buddy, you're so funny…and cute.

This is my chance. I look at the clock. Only one minute to seal the deal.

"Melanie, will you go with me to the party tomorrow night?"

She looks at me…

Buddy!

Our Special Ed teacher Mrs. Stevenson calls me up to her desk.

How old are you?

"Sixteen."

What do you want to do when you leave high school?

"I think I want to be Prime Minister."

Everyone laughs, especially Melanie.

What's so funny?

She points a crooked finger at the large red F on my mid-term exam.

With grades like this, you would be lucky to land a job as a janitor. Besides, you can't be Prime Minister.

"Oh, yeah, why not?"

Well, for one thing, you're bla —

"I'm what?"

I don't know any politicians who are as, flamboyant as you. You might make a half decent actor…or something.

"Oh, yeah? Will my flamboyant nature get me movie parts, you think?"

Big laugh.

If you don't smarten up, young man, you won't have a choice in what you do. You will be a loser all your life. Is that what you want?

"Yeah, I want to be a loser."

On the way back to my desk I whisper to Melanie.

"I'm so getting out of here."

   The bell rings.

She hands me back the note.

I drink lemon gin.

She grabs her stuff and runs out of the class.

   Opens piece of paper.

She said yes!

Melanie McDougal loves me! She really, really loves me!

Oh, I'm keeping this note! I save all our correspondence. I hide them in a special envelope under my mattress with all my secret memories.

I'm on a bus headed downtown to the only barber on Main Street. I have to update my look for my new girlfriend.

"A Mohawk, please."

"Eww! It looks great! Is there any way for you to straighten it?"

"I love it."

Now I need a new outfit. I just got paid from the A&W. I can afford it.

Melanie wears army pants. These are perfect.

Black combat boots. She'll love them.

Ooo, this black fishnet top will go nicely over my favourite muscle shirt.

Oh, my God, a Michael Jackson Thriller Jacket. I've always wanted one!

I look great. Now all I need is some black eyeliner.

I throw my old clothes out and the new Buddy walks out of the store.

Wearing pants made for fighting put me in a tough mood.

"Dozer better watch his ass!"

◆

At home, my sisters Heckle and Freckle snicker when they see me. Well, they are obviously too young to have fashion sense.

In my room, I can't stop looking at myself in the mirror. We will be the talk of the school. I can just see it now. My date with Melanie will be perfect.

◆

I have a bouquet of flowers in my hand and I am casually leaning on the hood of my best friend Mike's Mustang.

I look sick. I'm wearing shades and uh, smoking a cigarette. Kinda like a black James Dean. Rebel with a cause. Oh, I'm bad.

Melanie comes out of her house. Our eyes meet.

She looks devastatingly sexy. My punk rock angel. She smiles that smile that would make the old Buddy blush, but the new me's too tough for that. I do lift the corner of my mouth though and snarl a bit. I nod my head back and forth. I like what I see.

Melanie saunters down the sidewalk towards me. The rumbling of the old Mustang's engine acts as our theme music.

She is standing directly in front of me now.

I hand her the flowers. A dozen red roses with the tips sprayed black.

They're beautiful, Buddy.

"Not as beautiful as you are."

I pull off my shades, revealing the black eyeliner smudged underneath my eyes.

Sexy! Dangerous! Bad!

You did all this for me?

"Yup, all for you."

Dozer would never do this for me.

"I know, baby. I know."

Ours eyes lock onto each other.

Oh, Buddy...

Oh, Buddy…

OH, BUDDY…

I love…

     Phone rings.

It's Mike — bootlegger, newly elected student council president and my best friend.

"Hey dog-breath…Yeah, I'm coming to the bush party, duh! Can I get a ride? Great… Oh, hey, can you pick me up a bottle of lemon gin on your way over? …Ooo, and some rye?…Oh, and can we pick up my date?… Yes, I have a date, you dick… Melanie McDougal… What's so funny?… Shut up!… Oh, shit! My mom and are dad home. I gotta go. They're going to freak when they see my hair…"

                         ♦

It's dinnertime and the whole family is sitting around the table. It's quiet, except for the sound of cutlery scraping against plates and my dad's grinding teeth. He won't take his eyes off my Mohawk. He drops his knife and fork and pushes his chair back.

You are doing the dishes tonight… alone.

He stomps down to the basement.

Well, at least I'm not grounded.

◆

It's the night of the party and my parents have left the house for the evening.

I do my chores, I run up stairs and hop into the shower. I pull out the blow-dryer and start drying my hair straight just like the barber did yesterday.

Forty-five minutes later, it looks like a cotton ball with flat sides.

Maybe the pants will help?

Shit. A broken zipper.

I throw on the rest of the outfit.

Still something missing. What does Melanie do that makes her look so ferocious? Oh, my God, I forgot the most important part, the black eyeliner.

I sneak into my parents' bathroom and open my mom's makeup drawer.

Ah ha, I knew she'd have one. Oh, it's brand new. Deep Night. Mmm…

I'll just borrow it. I'll put it back before she even realises it's missing.

I can't do it. Every time I put the pencil near my eyes they just start leaking.

I wash it away repeatedly with soap and water.

I finally manage to put a thick line underneath each eye.

One last look in the mirror. The tears have made the liner run down my cheeks.

Honking horn.

Shit, Mike's here. Oh, I give up.

"Don't say a word, Mike! It's called style! Not something I expect you to know anything about."

Car takes off.

Girls don't drink lemon gin unless they want to get laid. I boughtcha beer.

"But she hates beer, Mike! She says it makes her bloated."

Car screeches to a stop.

"Ah, there she is. Eww, she looks great."

Dude, she looks crabby.

You're late. I hate it when people are... What have you done to yourself? Did you know your fly is down? Oh, I have to be home early.

    Car screeches off.

We drive up to the bush party.

My eyes are still stinging and I have tears running down my cheeks.

Mike stops the car. Without a word, Melanie hops out and walks over to a group of girls standing around the fire.

Mike gets out.

Here's her beer. Here's your rye. Dude, you have black shit on your face and you owe me twenty bucks.

He turns and leaves me standing alone.

"Hey, Melanie."

The girls she is talking to go quiet and their mouths fall open when they see me.

Ah...did you bring me my lemon gin like I asked?

"See, here's the funny thing, Mike went to the liquor store for me. He bought you this instead."

Great. A warm beer.

"Drink it. The whole case is for you."

Do I look like I wore my fat pants to the party?

The girls giggle and turn their backs.

I open my bottle of rye. The first gulp burns my stomach.

"Drink up, Mel. Here, I'll open you another one."

Don't bother, Buddy.

"Aww, come on, Mel, I want you and I to have a good time tonight."

And I want a BMW. I've learned to live with disappointment.

I put my hand on the small of Melanie's back. To pull her closer.

    Slap.

Don't touch me, Buddy! I'm not your girlfriend! I don't date boys who wear makeup, you weirdo.

Everyone around the bonfire is staring at us.

I find Mike sharing a bottle of lemon gin with Stephanie Wilcox.

"Mike, let's get outta here."

Now?

"Mike, I gotta get out of here."

Good luck finding a ride.

I am really drunk now.

SFX: *Did you see the faggot? etc.*

Melanie looks across the bonfire. There, staring back through the flames, is Dozer.

He waves at her.

She waves back.

She nods towards me and rolls her eyes.

He throws his head back and laughs.

Melanie whispers something to her girlfriends, then looks at me and pats me on the shoulder.

She hopes I find what I am looking for. She hands me her beer and walks away.

I can see Melanie and Dozer through the flames. He smiles at her. She smiles back. He reaches out and gently strokes her angelic cheek. They kiss.

I turn and look at the girls Melanie was talking to. They're just staring at me.

I feel something. I don't know what it is.

◆

I wake up on the floor in my closet. I wipe the drool off my chin. How did I get here? I can hear my mom and dad yelling.

Which one of you took the black eyeliner out of your mother's makeup drawer?

"Oh, no!"

I was supposed to put it back before she even realised it was missing.

I run down and burst into my sister's room.

My dad's hand is in the air, ready to strike.

"Oh, my God, Mom! I found your eyeliner."

You did? Where?

"It was stuck in Mom's hairbrush!"

Buddy, that doesn't make sense.

"Well, it's true. I just opened the drawer and there it was."

Pause.

Don't lie to us!

"I'm not."

That's it. Go get the belt.

Get my belt.

Buddy, get my belt now!

The only way out of this is to change the subject. What can I say that will make them feel sorry for me and save my butt at the same time? Think, Buddy! Think! Think! Think!

Buddy, why would you steal the eyeliner out of my makeup drawer?

"Because I'm a fag!"

That's no excuse!

Dad storms out.

SLAM.

Why on earth…?

"I just wanted a girl to like me, Mom."

And you picked makeup to do it?

"Yup."

And the hair and the clothes?

"Yup."

Did it work?

"Nope."

Buddy hands her the liner.

You keep it. It was a bit young for me anyway, don't you think?

I place the liner in my special envelope with all my secret memories.

◆

Monday after the bush party. I am walking into the school.

Mike comes up behind me and cuts me off.

I need to talk to you.

"Oh, hey, Mike, I got pretty wasted at the party, huh?"

Dude, you can't go into school.

"What are you talking about?"

We saw you!

"Saw what?"

We-saw-you!

"Ew, Mike, you're spitting on me. I gotta get to class."

He slams me against the wall.

Listen, Buddy. We saw you! At the party! With that guy! We followed you into the bushes. I saw you… We all saw you, Buddy!

"I can't breathe."

I've always stood up for you. When everyone else called you faggot, I said no. No, he's not…and now? Fuck! You were my best friend. How do you think this makes me look?

"I gotta get to class."

Don't bother, man. There was a meeting.

"What meeting?"

Student council…and we decided that you are no longer welcome in this school.

"You're nuts, Mike. Get out of my way."

Go ahead. Go… But I'm doing you a favour here… If you go in…you may not make it back out.

"You're serious?"

Dead serious.

"I thought you were my friend, Mike."

I can't be friends with a fag, Buddy.

He turns around and walks into the school.

◆

My suitcase is packed and ready beside me.

I think they've finally gone to bed.

I'm getting out of here.

It's not you, it's him — Age 8

BUDDY (as the doctor): *Take a deep breath in… And out…*

I am sitting on the doctor's table while my mom and dad watch him examine me.

Mom can't sit still and her cheeks are turning red.

Dr. Lucas, do you have Buddy's test results?

In…

And out…

Dad is just staring at the doctor like a zombie, and grinding his teeth.

The doctor lifts me off the table.

You may put your shirt back on, Buddy.

Dr. Lucas sits in his big leather chair with the gold buttons.

I just have a few questions before I get into the test results.

> *Pause.*

Buddy is adopted?

Yes.

At what age?

He was two.

And he's eight now.

"But I'll be nine in three weeks."

Buddy. This is a conversation just between your parents and me.

Mom reaches over and squeezes my hand. She knows I don't like Dr. Lucas.

Now, it says in his medical records that he is mixed race. What does that mean, exactly?

His mother was white and his father was a Negro man from Trinidad.

I see.

Mom looks at me, then back to Dr. Lucas

Doctor, what does that have to do with my son's bedwetting problem?

What! I didn't know we were here to talk about that!

Dr. Lucas takes off his glasses.

There may be consequences from an interracial union.

Mom looks at Dad. He's just staring forward.

What are you saying, doctor?

All right, I'm just going to tell you how I see it… Buddy's lazy. This is no reflection on you as his parents. You are doing the best you can for him. He is lucky that you chose him, frankly. But Buddy is lazy. Plain and simple. Hence his poor academic performance and his unwillingness to get out of bed to go to the bathroom.

     Pause.

Mom crosses her legs.

Ok, what do you suggest his father and I do about it, then?

Discipline. Wake him up every night. If he has wet the bed, make him change the sheets.

In the middle of the night?

Yes, and every night until Buddy learns and the bedwetting stops.

Dad is going to break a tooth if he doesn't stop grinding his teeth.

Dr. Lucas turns to me.

And you, young man, are to have nothing to drink after four in the afternoon. Is that understood? That way there will be nothing in you to pee out in the middle of the night.

The doctor closes the file and smiles at me.

You can do this, Buddy. If not for you, do it for the people who have sacrificed so much so that you could have a good life. Will you do that for me?

Uh huh.

Good boy.

The doctor stands.

Good luck.

Dad stands.

Mom stands.

Say thank you, Buddy.

"Thank you…sir."

◆

We are in the car. I am in the back seat.

At the first stop light, Dad looks at Mom.

I told you he was lazy.

They think it's me.

I want to steal something now. Once the feeling starts, I can't stop until I take something from someone. It doesn't have to be expensive. The smaller, the better. Slip it into my pants pocket when no one is paying attention.

Money is my favourite thing to take. I can spend it right away on the candy I like. Helps me get rid of the evidence and no one can prove anything. I know it's wrong, but it makes me feel good.

Father, by the way… — Age 35

BUDDY: "Hi, Andy…? Andy…it's… Buddy… You know? Buddy…from Vancouver. I called before… I'm your birth son…"

"I am great. I just wanted to wish you happy… And you? How are you doing…? Good! I'm glad! So, Andy, are you busy at the moment…? Ok. I don't want to disturb you. Did you get that copy of my adoption papers I sent you a few months ago…? And? What do you think…? Well, about the papers. Me. Me and you. I mean, you being my birth father…"

> *Pause.*

"You haven't…? How long ago did you get them…? Do you mind that I am phoning you then? I don't want anything from you… No, I just want you to know that I am very happy with the family I have."

"I want to know some things about you. What your life has been like. I don't know what it is like to have blood relatives…black relatives. My adoptive family is white…"

"I Googled your name… Yes. Very impressive résumé… Yeah, I'm an actor too… Was it hard finding work as an actor in the 70's…? There weren't a lot of black parts on Canadian television…"

"I went to a theatre school in Alberta… Well, I started out doing plays, but I've landed some film and TV parts…I've started writing. I love it… I do find that I am very sensitive to criticism, though. I think I need to get a thicker skin… I don't know. I want to learn. I ask people their opinions and I get overwhelmed with the responses. It's kinda stupid, really…"

Pause.

"You are so right, opinions are like assholes…and they all stink…Wow! Thanks, Andy…that's very good advice… I've been pretty fortunate, actually… Well, my last movie was with Halle Berry…I played her gay co-worker… Yes, I am gay…"

An uncomfortably long pause.

"Hello…? Andy…? Andy, are you there…? Well, I guess I should go then."

"So. Would you be open to us meeting face-to-face one day…? God willing? God willing…"

"Well, thanks for taking the time to talk to me, Andy. Oh, and by the way… happy Father's Day."

Dial tone.

Oh, brother! — Age 20

BUDDY (as his agent, Frank): *Not a lot of parts out there for someone of your type. Casting tends to be very…stereotypical. You may not be black enough for many of the roles out there. If you could learn to be more ghetto, this may open the door for you.*

Frank is my first agent. He said yes to me when everyone else said no, but he's short and has a bad comb-over.

I have an audition for you. It's a perfect part. Don't fuck it up.

He walks me to the door

Oh, and one more thing — do you have be so gay?

◆

Ten pages! Holy shit. 20-25 year old, African-American, with boy-next-door looks, but a street kid's view of the world.

Hmm, sounds good so far.

Little Bra is…wait a second, is his name really Little Bra?

Yup. Ok. Different.

Little Bra is a talented…rapper/drummer/gangster.

You're kidding.

Little Bra lives with Kimberly. They have a sexual relationship that turns abusive. Five sex scenes… One attempted rape… Please suggest actors who can rap and play drums…?

No. No. This must be a mistake.

I pick up the phone.

"Hey, Frank, it's Buddy. Dude, I think you gave me the wrong audition."

I did? What is the character's name?

"Umm, Little Bra."

No, that's the part, all right. You sound upset.

"I don't play drums and I have never rapped in my life."

You haven't?

"No. What made you think I did?"

You're black.

"Dude, are you kidding me right now?"

I can cancel. But you will quickly get a reputation for being a moody actor. I don't think you want that…

"No, I don't."

Ok then, Buddy, suck it up. Call me tomorrow when you are done.

◆

I have decided to commit, to give this audition all that I have. I am an actor. I can do this.

I rummage through my closet, looking for clothes my women-raping, drum-beating, lyric-spewing, rapper slash gangster would wear.

The only rapper I can think of at the moment wears over-sized army pants. I used to own a pair of those when I was in high school. At the bottom of a box marked Burn This, I find them wrapped around a pair combat boots, a fishnet top and my Michael Jackson Thriller Jacket.

Now I have a whole costume. Getting more gangster all the time.

Ok, what to do with my hair? Rappers wear bandanas, don't they?

All right—looks good. I mean—I don't look like a black man—more like a member of the gay Mexican drug cartel. But I look good. I mean bad, really bad. Scary even.

I'm ready!

◆

On the way to the audition I glare at the other people on the bus. Who's bad? I'm bad. I'm so getting this part.

◆

I pause for just a second outside the audition waiting room. Breathe. Breathe. You got this. Now go in there and nail it!

The room is packed. The only empty spot is on a couch between two very large football player types.

I ignore the mumbles and the snickers as I quietly make my way through the room.

"Excuse me, guys."

Every face staring at me is not just black, but that kind of black that is almost blue. All the guys are at least 6 feet tall. Not one of them is dressed in costume. Most are in slacks or in jeans. One guy wears a baseball hat to one side. That's as crazy as it gets.

As I look around the room filled with jive-talking black men, I realise I am the whitest guy here.

The casting agent is glaring at me.

Are you Buddy?

"Um—yes."

Well, I guess you can read.

Ok.

Action!

"I gots money in my pockets
The girls they want to sock it
My swagger so fly
Makes the other nigggas want to
Die de die de die de die die
I got ice on my grill
Cristal on the chill
I'm a mean motha fucka
Don't mess with me brother
Unless you wants to
Die de die de die de die die
Bam."

"Would you like to see anything else?"

Well, that was awkward.

As I shut the door, I hear the room break out in laughter.

♦

I am sitting on the bus. Everyone is staring at me. I can't look at them.

What am I going to do? Are these the only roles I can go out for? Because if this is the case, I'm done.

I hear the phone as I unlock my door.

What the fuck? What happened? I just talked to the casting agent. That was a great part and you blew it! Mega Artist Management can no longer represent you. Sorry.

    Dial tone.

Why bother? — Age 29

BUDDY: I can't look at the cop. If I do, I know I will say too much.

Do you understand these rights as I have read them to you?

"Yeah."

Again I should remind you that this is being recorded. We know what you did. Theft from an employer is deemed highly offensive. You were in a position of trust and it takes a certain amount of planning and manipulation to steal from someone you work for. Judges don't look kindly on it. They tend to hand out stiffer sentences. Three years, I would think, possibly more. Please think before you speak. Would you like something to drink before we begin? Water, Coca-Cola …

"Coke, Coca-Cola."

The door closes.

I can't breathe. This can't be happening to me. Don't panic. Get a lawyer. They'll be able to get you out of this. Stop shaking, you'll look guilty. Don't give them anything that they can use against you. Just keep your mouth shut. Make them prove it… I wonder what they know…

The door opens.

"I did it. I stole the money. I was going to put it back. I did it. I was gonna stop. So what happens now?"

Explain to me. What did you do?

"I've been stealing money out of the till."

How much money?

"I don't know, a lot."

How did you do it?

"Um…well…the customer would come into the store to buy something… I would pocket the money instead of putting it into the till."

For how long?

"Since I started, I guess. Six months, maybe longer."

What did you do with the money?

"I don't know…buy stuff."

What kind of stuff?

> *Buddy shrugs his shoulders.*

Well you must have spent it on something. What was it?

> *Pause.*

Drugs?

"Yes… drugs… I can't stop. I've tried. I have. I was going to quit the job last week before I got caught, but I didn't. I need some help, I guess."

You guess?

"I need some help."

So, get help.

"Why bother, right?

Why bother?

"There's no point. I'm sick."

So, get treatment.

"Is there treatment for being gay? How 'bout black?"

You know, just because you're black and gay doesn't give you the right to be a loser. Are you close to your family?

"I used to be."

What's the issue?

"I don't know…my dad and I don't see eye to eye anymore. We just don't talk."

Ya know, Buddy, there's a saying in my line of work.

"What's that?"

No change happens without somebody getting arrested first.

"Oh, yeah…that's funny"

Your parents should really know what is going on.

"Ok."

I am going to need you to write a statement.

"Ok."

I can't tell you what to write, but don't leave out anything out that you have told me. I'll get you a pen and paper. I think that under all this there is still a nice guy somewhere.

> *The door shuts.*

"Is there?"

Not a good time — Age 34

BUDDY: This envelope is so thick.

I can't stop shaking.

I can't look.

Once I read this there is no going back.

I kinda like being the man who came from nowhere.

I told myself that I didn't really care to know about my birth family.

Now that I have the papers, I realise I do want to know. I've always wanted to know. I've just never let myself have any sort of hope.

Ok. Breathe. Breathe.

Actor reads only underlined portions of the letter.

This letter is in response to your Request for Release of Information application and also acknowledges receipt of your Post-Adoption Registry application.

Enclosed please find information from the Adoption Orders, (certificates and documents sealed under Section 74.1 (2) of the Child, Youth and Family Enhancement Act. While we realise that some of the documents may not be entirely legible, please be assured that we have printed the best copy we were able to obtain from the adoption records.)

Your birth mother has vetoed the record; therefore, we are not able to provide you with any identifying information about her. She did, however, provide a written statement including medical information, which we are forwarding to you.

So what does this mean?

Dear Buddy,

My feelings surrounding this "Disclosure of Information" are so mixed with emotions. I hope you can understand the difficulty back then. I was an 18-year-old white girl having a black man's child in central Alberta. I would like to meet you and explain face to face, but I feel the need to protect my existing family. This is not a good time in their lives or mine to proceed with full disclosure.

As for medical information, I can tell you a few things. My siblings and myself are all healthy. My mother has suffered two strokes and one heart attack in recent years, but she is eighty-three years old. My father unfortunately passed away from leukemia the year you were born.

Wow.

One main concern would be that one of my children has Insulin Dependent diabetes. My family also has a history of learning disabilities. Not fully diagnosed, but explained as overt or slight Attention Deficit Disorder as well as a reading for meaning disability.

So that's where I get it from.

Since the moment you were born I have hoped and prayed for a good life for you.

I wish you well,

Your Birth Mother

> *On the phone.*

"Hi, Mom, it's me.

Can you get Dad on the phone too?

Hey, Dad.

I got my adoption papers.

She said no.

I know.

I know.

I knew there was a possibility of rejection. It doesn't make it any easier.

Listen, I'm gonna go. I'll call you tomorrow.

I love you guys too.

I gotta go, but I'll call tomorrow

Love ya, bye."

I place the papers in my secret envelope.

I wish you well.

Tassels - Age 7.5

BUDDY: There is a knock at my bedroom door. I manage to hide the skipping rope behind my back as my dad opens it.

"Dad! I thought we said that when I turn seven, you would knock and I would say come in."

I don't remember that agreement.

"I need my privacy, Dad!"

Buddy, you and I made plans to watch Roots *on TV tonight. 8:00. You, me… Roots…and a big bowl of popcorn. Don't forget.*

"Great. I can't wait!"

♦

I'm actually seven-and-a-half years old and my sister just gave me her bright pink skipping rope.

I'm moving on, she said.

It has multi-coloured metallic tassels on each handle. I love these tassels. I love the rubbery smell it leaves on my hands after I skip. I love how I can stretch it out till the bright pink of the rubber turns to white then back to pink when I release it. I love the way I can see the shiny tassels twinkling when I skip. I love my skipping rope!

I take it down into the basement when no one else is around and practise. It is mine and mine alone. It takes my mind off my problems and is an excuse for me to run away and be by myself.

It sits and waits, tucked away in a secret pocket in my school knapsack. At the drop of a hula hoop, any moment — as long as no one's watching — I take out my pink, brightly tasseled rope and skip till I need a puff on my inhaler. I can get up to 150 now.

Darlene Boyle is toast.

◆

Since I was a baby, my father has carried me around on his shoulders.

When you are up there, I feel like a king, he says.

I hold onto his forehead with my small hands to steady myself as he lifts me up and carries me to the living room for the beginning of the ground-breaking miniseries, *Roots*.

Do you remember what this show is about?

"Black people."

And?

"Africa?"

What else?

"Slavery, Daddy?"

That's right. A long time ago people like you were brought to America and forced to work for free. Off you get.

"How come?"

Because they had darker skin.

"So if I was living back then, I would be a slave?"

Yes. Buddy, there are people who may not like you because you are different.

"No way!"

Do you want something to drink?

"Umm, some Kool-Aid, please."

I watch the introduction of *Roots* with deepening curiosity. I am excited to see a TV show filled with black people.

Dad returns with the bowl of popcorn and my drink.

We sit and watch all the episodes together.

At first I feel uncomfortable watching the black people living in Africa. Everyone walks around almost naked. Boy...am I glad to be Canadian. Everyone has to wear shirts to school here.

I am surprised to see black people kissing and acting like my white parents.

"Did you and Mommy buy me, Dad?"

No, we adopted you.

"Did you change my name the way Kunta Kinte became Toby?

No, your name has always been Buddy.

"Did you want a Negro boy?"

We wanted a little boy. We didn't care what colour you were. As long as we got to love you.

It's late, way past my bedtime, and Dad is tucking me in.

"Am I a Nigger, daddy?"

No! You're not! And if anyone ever says anything like that to you I want you to let me know. Promise?

"I promise."

Now get some sleep. I love you.

"Love you more."

◆

I know every element of grade four skipping; Chinese Skipping, Double Dutch and Spanish Dancers. I can go salt and pepper. I can go backwards, forwards — and even crisscross. Oh, I am good.

At school I watch the girls skip at recess, to check out my competition. Envy seeps out of every pore because I can't join them. Because everybody knows boys don't play with girls. Even I know that. Me skipping with girls at recess would mean me getting beat up after school. I'm not gonna give Nelson Weaver another chance. He already thinks I'm a freak.

Darlene Boyle is the best skipper. She's a tall farm girl who always has food stuck in her braces. But I know I'm better than her.

I always ignore the urge to skip with the girls, until today. Today my best friend Christine asks me to come and join them. I don't even think twice. I leap to my feet. I practically fly into the middle of the long spinning rope.

Spanish Dancers do a kick, kick, kick!
Spanish Dancers do the splits, splits, splits!
Spanish Dancers turn around, round, round!
Spanish Dancers get out of town!

I did it. My first time! It was a perfect entrance, a stunning exit, and I knew every move!

Christine says I am as good as Darlene. Then she says... *there should be a skip-off!*

Before I can say no, she grabs Darlene, who says—

There's no way. We'll see about that. Well, what are you going to skip with? That booger hanging out of your nose?

"No, as a matter of fact, Darlene, I have my own rope."

Well, go get it then. Let's see your skipping.

There's no way out. Not with all the girls watching and I *know* I can beat her! I reach into the secret pocket in my school knapsack and pull out my pink, tasseled rope.

Pepper... Backwards... On one foot! Ready?

"Oh, I am so ready."

Oh, you are so going down.

"One...two...three...four...five..." I'm doing it!
"Nine...ten...eleven...twelve..." This is a piece of cake!
"Sixteen...seventeen...eighteen...nineteen...twenty...twenty-one...twenty-two...twenty-three...twenty-four...twenty-five..." She's getting tired—
"Thirty...thirty-one, thirty-two, thirty-three..." Her foot catches on her rope but she keeps going—
"Forty...forty-one...forty-two..." God, I love these tassels!

"Fifty…fifty-one…fifty-two…" Oh my God, Darlene Boyle's going down! I'm still going strong! I'm gonna win! I'm gonna win! The girls are all cheering me on!

Then I see Nelson Weaver heading towards us.

Look, guys. Toby's skipping like a fag!

"My name isn't Toby, Nelson."

Yes, it is. It's your slave name.

All the girls go quiet.

Your real name is Kunta Kinte!

> *Nelson shoves Buddy to the ground.*

I can feel every stare. I just lie at Nelson's feet. Frozen. My skipping rope twisted around my legs. I can't move. Nelson bends down and yanks at the skipping rope.

Good to see you brought this with you today. Come on, guys, you hold him down while I teach this Nigger a lesson.

The girls move away and the group of boys advance.

He flicks my rope in the air.

What's your name, slave?

"You know what my name is, Nelson."

No, I want you to say it! I want you to say 'My name is Toby'! Say it or I'll whip you like a slave!

He flicks my skipping rope again and it nicks my cheek — but I grab it — and I don't let go.

Nelson pulls—and I don't let go.

He jerks it hard—and I don't let go.

He starts to walk backwards pulling me along the ground—and I don't let go.

The skipping rope starts to stretch, till the bright pink of the rubber turns to white—and I don't let go.

> *Bell rings.*

I let go. And run.

◆

I sit at my desk with my head in my arms so no one can see me cry.

There's a tap on my shoulder. It's Darlene. She hands me my rope. Most of the tassels have been torn off and it's covered in dirt, making the bright pink rubber look dull and lifeless.

You're going to need this to skip with us tomorrow.

"Thanks, Darlene."

Nelson's in the desk behind me.

Yeah, I'm gonna need it when I beat you up after school.

Five minutes before the bell rings, I tell the teacher:

"I have to meet my mom out front for a doctor's appointment."

Even though I don't have a note, she lets me go.

I run down the hall and out of the school.

I pass a garbage can and I toss the skipping rope in.

I look back one last time. What's left of the sparkly tassels catches the light. A breeze moves it. It looks like it's waving to me.

◆

I sit on the edge of my bed and chew on my nails. They are bleeding, but I don't stop.

I hear my dad's car pull into the garage. I hear him enter the house. I hear his heavy footsteps on the stairs.

He knocks on my door.

"Come in."

Hey, Buddy. How was school today?

I can't lift my head to look at him. If I do, I know I will start crying.

Your mom said that you barely said hello when you came home. You didn't even ask for a chocolate chip cookie. That's not like you.

My lip starts to quiver but I still don't say anything. Dad comes and sits on the bed beside me and pulls me onto his lap.

He moves my chin up with his finger till our eyes meet. I can't control myself any longer and bury my face in his chest. Between giant sobs, I tell him everything.

◆

It's dinnertime. I am quiet. I can't eat. Dad keeps looking at me. He doesn't say anything.

I get up to start the dishes.

Your sisters will do your chores for you tonight. Go down and get your coat.

I do so without saying a word.

The car ride is silent except for the sound of the engine and my dad's grinding teeth. He only grinds his teeth when he is mad.

He stops the car in front of a rundown house. All the lights are on and I can see everyone inside is sitting down eating dinner.

Keep your head up the whole time. Don't look at your shoes. Don't look around you. Don't be afraid. Do you remember what we talked about?

"Yes."

We get out of the car. I walk up the sidewalk behind him, dragging my feet. I feel sick to my stomach.

Dad waits for me at the front door.

He puts his arm on my shoulder.

Ring the bell, Buddy.

A big, tall man opens the door and asks what we want.

Is Nelson here?

The big man tells us Nelson is in the middle of dinner.

This will only take a second, my dad says, pulling me in front of him so that I am now standing just inside the doorway.

The man calls out. We wait. It feels like forever.

Nelson comes up behind Mr. Weaver.

I just keep staring forward. Like my dad told me.

Nelson's mouth falls open when he sees me.

I clench my fists but look him straight in the eye.

My legs are wobbly but I look him straight in the eye.

I pull away till I don't feel my father's hand on my shoulder anymore, and look him straight in the eye.

"Nelson, don't you call me a Nigger or a fag ever again."

Nelson looks at his father then back at me.

There is a long, uncomfortable silence, father staring at father, son staring at son.

Okay.

Mr. Weaver asks my dad how he knew where Nelson lived.

I'm a cop. It's a small town. Have a good night.

After the door closes, my dad bends down and lifts me onto his shoulder. I hold onto his forehead with my small hands to steady myself.

I'm so proud of you, Buddy. I think you deserve a treat after that. Tomorrow I'll take you to a toy store. What'cha think you're gonna get?

"A skipping rope, Daddy."

Oh, yeah, what colour?

"I think…a blue one this time…bigger tassels!

About the playwright

Berend McKenzie is an award-winning actor, writer, and producer, who currently lives in Vancouver, BC. His first play, the outrageous queer puppet show for adults, *Get Off the Cross, Mary!,* premiered at the 2006 Edmonton International Fringe Festival and won the Hero Award for Best Live Performance 2008. As an actor, Berend has worked with Oscar winners Halle Berry and Angelina Jolie.

Interview

In November of 2006, actor and comedian Michael Richards went on a rant at the Laugh Factory, calling members of his audience "niggers." In March 2007, while speaking at CPAC (American Conservative Action Conference) conservative commentator Anne Coulter called then Vice Presidential candidate John Edwards a "faggot."

After both instances there was a debate on CNN about whether or not the words faggot and nigger should be banned from the English language. The NAACP (National Association for the Advancement of Coloured People) saw fit to hold a funeral for the word nigger.

At first I was all for banning the words. While reflecting on my own experiences being the target of racism and homophobia I wondered how I could tell my own stories if these words could not be used. How could I learn about slavery and the true struggles of the queer community if those who have come before me were not allowed to use the words nigger and fag to tell their own stories?

This was the genesis for *NGGRFG*.

My goal was to write short stories that gave snapshots of what my personal relationship is and was with the words nigger and fag. Because these experiences, often painful, were pulled from my own life, reliving them proved to be more difficult than expected.

I wrote the first incarnation of the show in about seven months and it was comprised of four stories: "Liner," "Oh, Brother," "Father, By The Way," and "Tassels." The first story I wrote and the last one in the finished play was "Tassels." This story is where the intersection of homophobia and racism meet and is the emotional high point of the play.

The process of rehearsal happened at two separate times with two different teams. The first incarnation of the play was a co-production between Small Brown Package Productions (Vancouver) and Guys In Disguise (Edmonton). We workshopped the piece for one week about two months before the Edmonton premiere.

Performing the play for the first time was terrifying. There was a moment just before I stepped out onto the stage when I realised that there was no going back, and that the success of the show depended upon me. If I screwed up, there was nothing or no one that could help me.

Two years later I sent the play to Allen MacInnis at the Young People's Theatre in Toronto. Allen felt that there may be more stories to tell and offered to workshop the piece with the full backing of YPT. I was surprised to find that I did have more to say and over the following year added three new stories. "It's Not You, It's Him," "Why Bother," and "Not A Good Time."

Switching from writer to actor has been pretty simple. My biggest challenge was re-memorizing the new version of the play. My brain has an amazing way of storing certain lines of the show and if those lines have been cut or changed I had trouble finding the next beat.

The great thing about this show is that each story can stand on its own. "Tassels," for instance, has been performed in elementary schools. For secondary schools we linked four stories together—"Liner," "Oh, Brother," "Father, By The Way," and "Tassels" — in order to fit the play plus a five to ten-minute talk-back into a seventy minute block.

Cassandra

by Briana Brown

Characters

CASSANDRA — a nine-year-old girl

Setting

The action takes place in Cassandra's bedroom, New Year's Eve

Production History

The original production was performed by Briana Brown and stage-managed by Katie Horrill. It was performed at the following venues:

FemFest: Prairie Theatre Exchange, Winnipeg MB, October 2007
Bad Dog Short Play Festival: Toronto ON, October 2006
Ottawa, London, Victoria, Vancouver Fringe Festivals, 2006

It was subsequently produced by SeriousFUN! Theatre Company at the London Fringe Festival in 2010, with a twelve-year-old actor in the title role:

DIRECTED by Shannon Scott
STARRING Ally Connelly

Playwright's Notes

- The use of words such as "like" or "soooo" in the script's vernacular are not meant to indicate a "ditzy" tone, but rather one of excitement.
- The playwright encourages those producing the play to update the year in which Cassandra's list was written and expires, to reflect the time in which the play is being produced.
- *Cassandra* was originally conceived to be performed by an adult actor.
- The playwright would like to thank Katie Horrill, Erika Maaskant, Shannon Scott, Rick Jongejan, Kim Sider, David Rotenberg, Hope McIntyre, Anusree Roy, Judith Rudakoff and the York University playwriting class. And, always and especially, Al and Jane Brown.

Prologue

On a black stage, we hear CASSANDRA *hum "Auld Lang Syne."*

Scene 1

CASSANDRA *marches into her bedroom, yelling out her door.*

CASSANDRA: That is shockingly close-minded of you, DAD! (*pulls out a pack of Popeye cigarettes and takes a distressed drag*) My parents don't understand me. My parents just don't understand anything. Like, we were just politely discussing the subject of my allowance and I said, "Five dollars for a week's worth of work is child labour and is illegal," which is a perfectly rational thing to say. But immediately my dad's like, "Oh, the crazy ideas you get — where do you hear these things? Chortle. Chortle. Chortle." And — and I said, "Dad, did you ever consider that perhaps I'm bright for my age and I actually understand the concept of child labour and that maybe you should be proud of me for making such a clever comparison?" And he said, in a very stern voice, "Not at the table, honey." Which reminds me. (*gets up and goes to her door again*) I hope you know that when I turn eighteen I'm moving to Reykjavík! (*returns to audience*) You could say I'm struggling to find my place in the world.

How do you do? I'm Cassandra. Cassandra Smith. Only child of Tanya [*pronounce: Tawnya*] and Jake Smith: Team Smith. My dad is a dentist and my mom is a flake—at least that's what Morgan calls these women on TV who remind me exactly of my mother. I live here with them in the Smith residence and feel suppressed by their desire to treat me like I'm six, when I'm actually nine. At least for another six hours and twenty-three minutes. After that it's …double digits. That is a very stressful time in a young woman's life.

She takes an exaggerated drag and sits on her bed.

CASSANDRA: And — okay. I know I'm only a kid — I mean, (*gesturing towards her pigtails*) look at me. I don't pretend to be a grown-up. Well… (*shyly sneaking cigarette out of sight*) most of the time. I understand that this is a phase of "Life" through which we all must pass. But just because I'm a child, doesn't mean I'm fragile or stupid. Morgan says my parents are just trying to protect me. But — but I don't understand why. I think it's pretty disadvantageous in the long run. I mean, isn't it better to just know the facts? Then at least you're not disappointed. And sometimes knowing the realities of Life as an adult can help you get through your Childhood.

Like, for instance, at school I — I don't have that many friends and I get made fun of a lot for getting good grades. But I don't mind it so much, because I know that when I grow up, and go to work as an executive accountant in a big company in, like, New York, where I wear a power suit and work fourteen hours a day without taking a lunch break and have virtually no social life whatsoever, I'll get to laugh at *them*. Because even though it was my real life goal to become a folk-rock genius, and even though I am probably going to become a passive-aggressive workaholic, I will still make more money than they do, which means I'm more successful than they are, which means I'm happier than they are. That — that's probably what's going to happen. But if I didn't realise that about the world, if I hadn't seen enough movies to know that it's the losers who always end up succeeding in life, then I don't know if I'd have the strength necessary to continue on through public education at this stage of my life. I — I might decide to be homeschooled. People do it. So that's one reason I'm glad that I understand things about the world.

It's also good to understand things about the world so that you aren't taken advantage of. Like my student body was recently taken advantage of. My *now* student council president — I'm only in grade four, but I do follow my student council politics for the grade eights — and I think it's very interesting that our student council president, Sarah Sloan, she only got in because she gave everybody candy. Like that's going to make her a good president. "Here, have some candy, vote for me!" Like, do you even want those votes? I wouldn't want those votes. But she did, and everyone voted for her because they were blinded by the candy, and now she's the president, and she never does anything, and the entire school is suffering as a result of their own ignorance. But maybe if everyone understood that that is a pretty common political tactic, then people would have thought twice before allowing candy to make their decisions, and Derek Millington would be president instead. Sure, he's not as popular, but he — he was a fine candidate. (*sighs*) And, like, Sarah Sloan's dad got all her posters made at his company and her mom helped her write her speech and they're just so *involved* in her *life!* Like BUTT OUT and get your own life already. Team Smith definitely has their own life.

And Team Smith definitely doesn't mind staying out of my life, which is why they always (*calling offstage*) GROUND ME! And I can't afford to be grounded right now. I have things to do. I'm a highly motivated individual.

And I know that it sounds like I have it all together, but it hasn't been easy. I didn't always view the world around me with such clarity and perspective. No. I used to be quite clueless—much like my poor, misguided peers and parents. It wasn't until almost exactly a year ago, when I stumbled upon one of my mother's abandoned Christmas gifts, that I began to see the world for what it really is.

> *She runs behind her bed and puts something behind her back. She slowly walks up to the audience again and reveals a book, with a grand gesture.*

CASSANDRA: It's called *Change Your Life!* — exclamation mark — by Dr. Claire Decker, MD. I read the whole thing, all 526 pages, between Christmas and my birthday last year — New Year's. New Year's Day, not New Year's Eve. That's right — a lifetime of hung-over parents telling me to "keep it down and get those pancakes away from me" every year on my birthday (*laughs awkwardly*).

But in only 5 easy steps, Dr. Decker shows you how to change your Life and how to make yourself the person you've always wanted to be and how to lead the life you've always wanted to lead. But they weren't that easy — the steps — and a lot of them didn't really apply, even when I substituted the word "work" with "school."

But it did help me to develop a list of goals which I vowed last New Year's Eve would be accomplished by my birthday this year, when I turn double digits. I thought that if I wasn't able to fix things by the time I reached double digits, then… it's all over. Because let's face it — people don't really change. Which is why I *can't* be grounded right now. Because this List is not comprised of school things, but *Life* things.

> CASSANDRA *uncovers a bristol board List, previously covered by a bedsheet. We see the title, and the numbers 1–3, with the actual list items covered individually*

CASSANDRA: (*reading*) List of Things to Achieve for a Successful, And Therefore Happy, Life. By Cassandra Smith. Dated, December 31, 2009. Expiration: January 1, 2011. So time is running out, and I have not yet finished a single task on my list! I'm not generally a procrastinator. I finish my schoolwork efficiently and on time. Maybe I'm just a procrastinator at Life. That is not a good thing to be at all! Oh, I can't be grounded right now! I need freedom in order to accomplish these tasks. I need to be able to do a lot of research. I need unlimited juice access. I need access to a telephone. I need a fresh supply of Post-It notes. I need different visual sources from which to draw inspiration. I need space and time. I need Krystal *not* to be my babysitter tonight!

(*Catching her breath*) You see, usually Morgan is my babysitter, and she is soooo cool. She's seventeen. She even acknowledges and respects my disagreement with the term "babysitter" and has agreed to call herself my "wayward companion" — like out of a novel by Jane Austen or the Brontë sisters. I love the classics. She says that she would still want to hang out with me even if my parents stopped paying her…but not as much. Which is fair. I appreciate her honesty. And she lets me stay up past my bedtime and watch grown-up TV with her, and explains to me everything that's wrong with it. Like how women are… (*difficulty pronouncing*) infantilized. She's really smart. And we critique commercials together, determining how they're trying to trick us, so that we won't be sucked in. And it's like she doesn't even mind hanging out with me at all. We spend a lot of time just sitting being quiet at the kitchen table while we both do our homework that involves writing. And then when we have "reading type" homework to do, or if we're not "totally swamped" — pleasure-reading, we move into the living room, with the TV *off*, and we sit on the chairs — but not like *in* them, kind of across them with our legs over the side like — (*tries to show the audience on her bed, very awkwardly fails*). But anyway, it's very cool, very outside the box. On June 28, which just happens to be the last day of school this year, Morgan goes to get her full licence, and she said that if she passes, she will come and pick me up from school that day. (*smiles*) Yeah.

But it looks like this just isn't my lucky day, because not only am I grounded for the most important night of my Life, but Morgan is at a 24-hour rally to protest the new Coca-Cola coffee shops, so she can't come over. So I'm stuck with Krystal. Krystal is definitely a flake. Krystal spells Krystal with a "K." All she cares about is boys and makeup and talking on the phone. She practically ignores me and then tries to send me to bed early. Like at the age of nine I still don't know how to tell the time? Especially when the clock in the kitchen is digital! I bet she's soooooooooo happy I'm grounded because now she doesn't even have to talk to me. She'll just sprawl out on our couch talking to her boyfriend Kris on the phone — also spelled with a K — and watch TV that (*still struggling*) infantilizes women.

Regardless, I am making an active decision to not let being grounded get to me. (*takes out her journal and begins writing*) You see, according to Dr. Decker — if you write down a resolution it helps it stay more firmly within you. (*mutters "not letting being grounded get to me" as she writes*). And I am not going to let Krystal get to me either. (*writes "not letting K-rystal get to me"*) I am a strong, capable individual and I have some major things to accomplish. Three major Life things. But there's no point in having a goal if you don't have a plan of action with which to fulfill it. And so, I have developed… A Plan of Action.

> *Cassandra reveals an entire "Life Betterment" office next to her bed, complete with binders, notebooks, Post-Its, highlighters and coloured tabs. She puts on a pair of glasses which have no lenses. She holds up a sheet of paper for the audience.*

CASSANDRA: As you can see, it outlines in detail how I can most successfully spend the remaining six hours of my single-digit-ness to achieve my goals. You see, according to Dr. Decker, "having an achievable list of goals and a detailed plan of action with which to achieve them are the most important steps to success." That and having a comfortable work environment. (*she looks around proudly*)

I don't know why my mom didn't feel the need to read *Change Your Life!* She never even noticed it went missing. I think Dr. Decker has some really salient advice to offer her readers. You have to be willing to let go of your pride, though, in order to enter a sphere of mental health. (*nods knowingly*) We're not all ready for that. I was ready, though. See — I'm good at school; I excel at academics, so I figure if I study Life and work hard at Life, then I should be able to excel in Life too. Get an A+. I guess Life is kind of like being homeschooled but without the shame. Now if I refer to my Plan of Action, it looks like it's about time to strike task number one off my List. (*revealing item #1 on her list*) Number One: Find and secure a suitable Life partner.

> *She retrieves a rotary telephone from under her bed, proudly showing it to the audience. She takes off her glasses.*

CASSANDRA: Shhh! I found it in the basement. I snuck it upstairs because I have a very important phone call to make. I have decided that there will be no more childishness between me and my true love, Derek Millington. I have read a lot about the subject, and I am definitely in love. I feel just like Catherine does about Heathcliff in *Wuthering Heights*. Here, I bookmarked the page.

> *She runs to retrieve her copy of* Wuthering Heights, *and proceeds to read, with epic gestures, and perhaps even a British accent.*

CASSANDRA: "My love for Linton" — not Derek Millington — "is like the foliage in the woods: time will change it, I'm well aware, as winter changes the tree. My love for Heathcliff" — Derek Millington — "resembles the eternal rocks beneath: a source of little visible delight, but necessary." (*stops reading and recites from memory*) "Nelly, I *am* Heathcliff! He's always, *always* in my mind: not as a pleasure, any more than I am always a pleasure to myself, but as my own being."

> *Having been "swept away," she looks up, embarrassed, and coughs slightly. Puts her glasses back on.*

CASSANDRA: But more importantly, it's a matter of practicality. I mean, I will soon be ten years old and have not yet had a boyfriend to stand next to at recess. Now, Derek Millington, like me, is very mature, and I think, if explained in the appropriate manner, he will see that a three-year difference in age is really insignificant when you're as well matched as we are. (Luckily, his birthday is in December so we're not a full four years apart.) I plan to explain the following similarities to him in an attempt to woo him. Point number one: we are both very intelligent. And even though we're both very intelligent, I think I am actually smarter than he is because I am, technically, "gifted," whereas he is merely geeky. Point number two — we have the same sense of humour. During his speech to become student council president, I was the only person laughing at his jokes. And no one usually laughs at my jokes either. Point number three — we are both lost and alone in the world. (*nods and continues without explanation*) Point number four — I think we could help each other's social standing. Me dating an older boy would definitely help my social standing. But he's going to be in high school next year, so he could just allude to this mysterious girlfriend that everyone would assume is in high school too — just a different high school. So he would be more popular too. I am going to tell him that we can date in secret until he reaches high school, if necessary. I'm willing to make that sacrifice for him. Like Romeo and Juliet. So! I am going to call him up and explain this all to him, so that we can move forward and through the stages of flirtation, courtship and love. If you'll excuse me, please.

> *She dials the phone, taking a very long time due to its rotary nature, and listens. She makes a slight sound like she is going to speak, stops, and hangs up.*

CASSANDRA: No answer.

> *A long pause, wherein she retrieves another Popeye cigarette.*

CASSANDRA: Do you hear that? Silence. You know my favourite part about silence is the fact that we never really experience *true* silence. Our version of silence just allows us to listen to things we can't usually hear.

See, 'cause nothing is simple. Not even silence is simple. People say it is, but anyone who knows anything about Life and the world knows that it's *not* simple. This world is a really stressful place to be alive. Sometimes I get so stressed out that I start to hyperventilate. I really do. I think it's genetic, because my parents do it too. I suppose the holidays are always stressful. And Christmas! An overweight man travelling the world in a single night to give gifts out of the goodness of his heart? Because he loves children? Well, what he should really do is adopt all the world's orphans, spend all that toy money on raising them, and let those of us who already have parents who give us gifts fend for ourselves. It's not that I'm not grateful… I just find his methodology to be a little ridiculous.

And I get really stressed out about school too. Like about how some kids get made fun of because they can't afford a designer backpack, or how it seems like it's always the really stupid people making all the important decisions (*clears throat*) — *Sarah Sloan* — or that the older girls at school, some of them…vomit after lunch. They do. Because they want to be as pretty as Miley Cyrus, but they've never heard of airbrushing. Which, by the way, is another reason I think it's really important in life not to be sheltered by your parents, and to take it upon yourself to understand how the world works. So you know about airbrushing!

> *She takes a final drag of her candy cigarette, throws it below her and stamps it out.*

CASSANDRA: But I still like the world. It's a fascinating place to be alive. Stressful, but fascinating. Like, if there was one thing I was more in love with than Derek Millington, it would be the world. (*getting excited*) I am utterly and completely in LOVE with this world! I — I think it's so interesting to see the way that Morgan's face changes when she talks about her boyfriend Neil, and I think it's so neat the way you can find out what's on TV on any given night just by riding the subway, and it's amazing that it's even a possibility that I have a penpal in Reykjavík. And I just think that the Saturday morning comics are hilarious! And I know there's so much left out there to explore! I — I wish there was a job where you could get to study *everything*. Like, absolutely everything — all about animals, and trees, and about the stars, and manufacturing, and learning different languages, and learning everything there is to know about China and Europe and the World Cup and every piece of music that's ever been written, and then the other part of your job would be to create music that's *never* been written! I know there isn't a job like that, but if there was, I'd want it.

Which is a foolish but apt segue into (*reveals*) Number Two: Make a firm decision about my future career. (*goes to get Dr. Decker's book*) Do you know what Dr. Decker says about your career? That it is *the* most important thing in your life. Because even after your friends desert you, and your children leave you, and your husband leaves you, you will still have yourself. And that "self" should be happy and fulfilled by what you do every day. And make money, so you can support yourself after you get abandoned.

I feel like I am very flighty about the career path I'm going to choose and that I should nail that down as soon as possible so I can focus. Get an internship or something. Am I too young for an internship? Yes. Well — yes. For me, being successful is the key to my happiness and I don't want to risk losing that. Hmm…maybe I could go to work for a big corporation and pretend that, like, my mom works there, so then whenever someone asks I can say, "oh, just heading to my mom's office". And then if they ask who my mother is, I'll just pretend I'm one of those unfortunate nine-year-olds who still doesn't realise that their parents have first names, and I'll look at them with a bewildered expression on my face, and say "Mom," and kind of shrug my shoulders. And they'll believe it. But then, I'll start helping people out — getting people's coffee, photocopying things, maybe highlighting some important documents in a warm shade of yellow. And, gradually, I'll become part of the office environment. Eventually, people won't even remember I said I had a mom because I will be so integral to the way that the office functions that they won't even care! That's a really good idea!

> *She retrieves her journal in order to write the idea down, pauses, and stops.*

CASSANDRA: But I—What I *want* to be … is a folk-rock genius. Well, a singer. I want to inspire people. I mean, I know that I never will and that I am much better suited to an office-type scenario, but if I was a singer… I would not do crack or other drugs. If I was a singer I would want to appreciate every second I was alive. Especially when I was on the stage.

> *In the following section* CASSANDRA *enacts all the moments she is describing — both what she would do, and how the audience would react. [Song Suggestion: Cat Stevens' "Peace Train"]*

CASSANDRA: Like, I would come out onto the stage, and bow in a gracious manner to the thunderous applause and screaming. And I would really try to connect with my audience. I would let them know I was glad they liked my songs. And then I would begin to sing… And then I would let my backup band keep playing and I would dance — but not choreographed like Miley Cyrus, but just really feeling the music…

> *She stops.*

CASSANDRA: It has to be about the music. If it's not about the music and you let the fame get to you, sometimes you go a little crazy. Like Cat Stevens. Morgan told me all about him. But, you know, I think he was pretty brave. When he wasn't happy with his Life the way it was, he renounced it completely and made a vow to change it. And he did.

I wrote a song about Derek. It's really embarrassing, I know. But as someone nearing their double-digit birthday I don't have a lot of life experience from which to draw. Like, I wrote a song about being grounded, but who wants to hear about that? I guess right now it's just practicing anyway so that by the time I'm seventeen I'm really good at writing songs — but then they'll be about seventeen-year-old things, so more people will want to hear them. Except my parents.

My life is definitely not songwriting material at the moment, though. If my life was a song at the moment, it would be one of those really sad songs, where someone is just pouring out their heart, but then it turns into a joke song.

She retrieves another Popeye cigarette.

CASSANDRA: Let me take just a moment to introduce to you the pathetic existence that is my Life. First, there's breakfast. Team Smith likes to start the day off right with the most perfect products available for consumption. It's an event. All breakfast, they talk about what great people they are for eating such a breakfast. Like, for instance, our eggs — are not just healthy due to their egg-like nature — but also because they are injected with something called "omega 3," which my mom thinks makes you a better person. Then we have *whole grain* toast, because that is currently the best kind of toast for you. Mom used to buy multigrain toast — well, bread — but then she discovered that everyone was lying, that multigrain toast is bad and whole grain toast is good. I think she felt deceived. Anyway, to finish off our balanced breakfast, we have a selection of *organic* fruit products which my mom cuts up in these slices and arranges them all nicely to ensure that within our fruit selection my dad and I have enough vitamin C and enough beta carotene and enough antioxidants to survive our day. All the while, Team Smith talks about how (*impersonating*) "Connie doesn't even *eat* breakfast in the morning," and how "Nancy and Bruce allow their children to watch TV during breakfast" and "isn't that horrendous?" At which point they take a brief moment to glance down the table at me and smile. But I might as well be watching TV for the amount of involvement I have in any of their conversations!

Then, every morning after breakfast, I have to go to the gym with my mom before she drops me off at school. And every day she and her friend Connie talk and talk and talk about how my dad is "solid," and how Connie's ex-husband is a "scumbag" and about their diets, and about new "articles" they've read in their health magazines. I used to stand in the workout area with my mom, sort of by the machines, trying to look casual. But it was so boring. I guess your body and your mind can't both be getting exercise at the same time. (*shrugs*) So now I just sit back in the change room and read. It's as good a place as any to get some serious reading done, I suppose. And right now I'm waiting with bated breath to see what will happen between Catherine and Heathcliff now that Catherine just cares about money and stupid Edgar Linton. It's devastating. And I guess it's better reading in the change room at my mom's gym than it is reading at school early in the morning. Getting caught doing something like that would not be good for my delicate social standing.

CASSANDRA: Which leads me to the worst part of my day — school. The people at school get me even less than my parents get me. Especially the girls. It's like they speak some sort of language that I — I just don't *get*. Like, for instance, on the last day of school before the holidays, I was in the washroom before recess when Jennifer M. — the prettiest and therefore most popular girl in our grade — says, "oh, guys, I'm sooooo fat. I'm so fat, guys". Then, Melanie, Stacy, and Jennifer L. each took turns saying in these high-pitched voices something like (*impersonating*) "No, you're not fat!" or "You're beeeauuutiful" or "Everyone in our grade wishes they were half as pretty as you." And then they all turned and looked at me with these scowls on their faces. Like, how could I possibly stand there washing my hands while Jennifer M. was having a crisis about her weight? How could I allow Jennifer M. to continue thinking she was fat? I didn't say anything. There wasn't anything I could add that the other three hadn't already covered... But then I realised that that's not what their scowls were saying at all. What their scowls were really saying was, "Can't you see we're having a private moment here about Jennifer M.'s weight, and won't you just leave already?" So I did. And I made sure to shut the door really fast behind me, because sometimes if I don't I can hear them talking about me before I even leave. And then they say things like why don't I just give up already and go get homeschooled.

CASSANDRA: But what they don't know is that I have a rebel inside of me just waiting to come out. I'm — I'm a...bomb waiting to explode! One of these days I'm going to surprise everyone. I'm gonna...I'm gonna to come to school wearing something crazy like, like this (*indicating her outfit*) — like, that I just like wearing when I'm alone in my room! And then I'll walk down the halls and I won't say hello to anyone. I'll just give them this look — like (*hesitant*)... "screw you." (*gasps, putting her hand over her mouth, elated*) And then I won't hand in my homework and I'll get an F and I won't even be upset! And then — I'll stand up on my desk (*stands up on her bed*) and I'll say, "Listen, everyone! I demand to be heard!" And everyone's eyes will get really big and focus in on me as they wait for my words of wisdom. And I will say, "Fellow students, Ms. Thomas..." (*stops herself, angry, and gets down off the bed*) Well, I would never really do that anyway. It's a slippery slope once you start down that path. I really need to work on my focus. I have less than four hours left to fix my life and here I am...ugh! Okay. List item number one. Phone call attempt number two.

She once again retrieves the rotary phone. She sits on her bed and places it on her lap. She dials, but before dialing the final digit she pauses.

CASSANDRA: "We have contained within us all the strength we'll ever need. It is just a matter of accessing it."

She dials the final number.

CASSANDRA: Hello, Mrs. Millington. This is Cassandra Smith calling. I attend elementary
school with your son Derek Milling— Derek. I was wondering if he is
perhaps available to speak for a moment? Yes. Thank you, Mrs. Millington.
(*pause*) Hello, Derek. This is Cassandra Smith calling — from Ms. Thomas'
grade four class. I was just calling to ask—if you would perhaps be—I was
wondering — if you would be interested—in . . . being my boyfriend. I know
this is a little unexpected, but I assure you, this is a good idea for both of us — a
very practical match. You see — (*pause*) Oh, I'm so sorry! Yes. (*begins turning
away from the audience in embarrassment*). Cassandra Smith. I wear my hair
in pigtails — it's brown. I laughed at all your jokes during your presidential
speech. (*pause*) Well, we could meet up in person then, if — (*pause*) But I
have a whole list of reasons — like we're both really smart. I'm very smart,
Derek. And I think you're funny. No one else thinks you're funny but me!
And I would be prepared to maintain our relationship outside of the public
eye — (*long pause*) Well, no, I don't understand, and I think you're missing a
really great opportunity, but I will respect your wishes. Bye-bye, Der—

> *She lingers, then quietly hangs up the phone. She is now completely
> turned away from the audience. A long pause. She turns slowly, and
> with a gesture of assurance to the audience ("it's okay") goes to the list
> and crosses out item number one.*

CASSANDRA: Number Two: Make a firm decision about my future career. Okay, I can do
that. I'll just do that right now. Okay, I want to be... a... corporate accountant.
There. That's my choice. It's practical, it will force me to see the importance
of math classes, my life will be filled with Post-Its and paper clips, which is a
good thing. It's a stable job, and it's pretty much guaranteed success because
I'm so driven. But — but I don't WANT to be an accountant. I ... I...

> *She fights for an alternative, then discouraged and disgusted, gives
> up. She crosses off item number two, then slowly reveals item number
> three.*

CASSANDRA: Number Three: Build a relationship with my parents. I tried really hard at
that one. I spent the whole year working on that one. I guess maybe I should
have worked on all three simultaneously. And I guess maybe I just should
have just been honest with them about how I always feel like a third wheel
in Team Smith: Volkswagen of Life. But instead I kept trying to prove that I
could be part of the Team. For months I have been trying to do an extra good
job of my chores, to start meaningful conversations with my mom before
we pick up Connie on our way to the gym, or to engage with my dad about
my teeth at the dinner table, showing that I too am appalled at the poor care
Krystal shows for her teeth. But they just weren't listening to me. It was like
I was speaking another language. And when I told Dad about my allowance
being like child labour, I was joking — I was making a joke. Showing that I
understood. But he just laughed at me like I couldn't possibly understand.
And like, how could he think that? I mean, how could he still not *know* that
about me? So after he said in his stern voice, "Not at the table, honey," I

replied, "If not at the table, then *when*? When? WHEN!" and I stood up on my chair. And then I got grounded. As usual.

And it's weird because it's like they care, but they don't *really* care. Like my mom makes sure I eat healthily so that when I'm forty I won't get cancer, but she won't listen to me when I try to tell her what I'm going to do at school *today*. And my dad was really nice and helped me make up a schedule for my allowance and even talked to me like a grown-up about "the responsibilities of saving" — but then when I tried to tell him my ideas for retirement and how I worry that the Canada Pension Plan won't be there for my generation, he just glazed over. Like, am I just boring? I'm an only child! I know how only children are supposed to be treated. I am supposed to be the centre of their universe! But instead of being the sun, I'm like some unnamed moon orbiting Pluto…which isn't even a planet anymore.

> *She thinks about this, then returns to her list, where she draws the final "x" on item number three.*

CASSANDRA: So I failed at everything on my list. And I know I'm grounded, but I can't help but see how appropriate it is that during this entire endeavour I have been completely alone. I have no one. I mean, Morgan — she's not a *real* friend. She can't be. Morgan likes me, that's true. And I think about that a lot. But you can only hang onto that for so long before you become painfully aware that the one relationship you're proud of is one where she's PAID to hang out with me! That's the lowest of the low when it comes to friendship hierarchies.

So last New Year's Eve as I sat alone in my room, finishing off the last pages of *Change Your Life!* and listening to my parents laughing downstairs with their friends, knowing I was going to wake up to yet another birthday with no friends and disengaged parents, I made a resolution. I decided it was time to get my head out of the clouds and get to work on fixing my Life. I thought, these are my formative years and if I don't create a good foundation I could end up like this for the rest of my Life. I'll *fail* at *Life*. So I switched on my reality sensor and set out to understand the world I was entering into.

But the problem is that everything around me is exactly the same as it was. With all of my facts and figures and understanding of "reality," I haven't managed to fix a single thing. The only thing that's changed is me. And I don't *want* to be like this! Sometimes I feel like if I am practical about one more thing I'll just stop breathing. I just want to be excited about things again — to be impressed when my dad makes a funny joke, or know it's okay if I get butterflies in my heart when I read *Wuthering Heights*—and not get upset with myself if I'm not in complete control every second of every day! I just want to run around and make funny faces and dance and sing and PRETEND things again! Because I'm good at that, and I like doing that, and I'm only nine years old! And even if I probably will end up wearing a power suit and telling people what to do for the rest of my Life, I at least want to *imagine* what it would be like to be a singer… Because maybe having dreams are just as important as whether or not they come true. And maybe they will come true. That's got to be a possibility, right?

Dr. Decker is right about one thing. You only have yourself. I can't depend on Morgan, or the girls at school, or Derek Millington, or my parents. I just have *me*. So I might as well let myself *be* me. And part of me — (*shyly*) a very well-developed part, I might add — is the part that dreams things.

> *She has an idea and gestures to the audience to "wait." She runs around her room, collecting various objects (the list, glasses, schedule, etc.) and places them in the middle of the room. She stands firmly behind the pile.*

CASSANDRA: I, Cassandra Smith, renounce the past year of my Life.

> *She steps over the pile.*

CASSANDRA: And very solemnly vow to be…(*a brief moment of panic, then victory*) whatever I want to be!

> *To finalize the moment, she tentatively begins to sing. [In the original production we chose the first two stanzas from Cat Stevens' "If You Want to Sing Out, Sing Out"]. Once vocally confident, she begins an awkward, but charming, sort of dance, feeding off the audience, ending in an exaggerated rock star pose. She calmly composes herself.*

CASSANDRA: Thank you.

> *She curtsies as the lights fade to black.*

About the playwright

Originally from rural Ontario, Briana spent several years in Toronto after graduating from York University (B.A. Honours, Theatre Studies). Her plays have been workshopped through Factory Theatre's LabCab Festival, Tarragon Theatre's Spring Arts Fair, Nightwood Theatre's Write from the Hip program, and the TheatreKairos writers' circle, where she subsequently took on the role of Program Director. She was commissioned by SeriousFUN! Theatre Company in 2009 to develop a script based on the experiences of the ten young women in its Going Pro program, entitled *The Line*. Also a theatre director, she directed her most recent play, *Almost, Again* (Toronto Fringe, Best of Fringe, 2010) which was included in the anthology *Out on a Limb*, edited by Kit Brennan (Signature Editions). She has directed productions at Theatre Passe Muraille's Buzz Festival, the Next Stage Festival, as well as the Paprika Festival's Tenth Anniversary Celebration (2010), *The Vagina Monologues* (V-Day Toronto, 2009) and assisted Brad Fraser on the Canadian premiere of *True Love Lies* (Factory Theatre).

Interview

Cassandra was my first. It was the first play I'd ever written start to finish and it was the first play that was totally my personal creation. But — and this is a huge "'but" — if I hadn't spent an entire summer performing it, you certainly wouldn't be reading it now.

Having just completed my undergraduate degree at York University, I decided to spend the summer of 2006 self-producing, performing, and touring a one-woman show to fringe festivals across Canada. The decision-making process went something like this: I started writing a play. I applied to a number of fringe festivals "just to see." I accepted entrance with the thought that I could always drop out. And then, suddenly, I was actually doing it.

And I am so very glad that I did.

I saw a huge number of productions that summer, some of which inspire me to this day. The woman brave enough to accompany me on the adventure, Katie Horrill (my stage manager), became a lifelong friend and collaborator. I was exposed to a wealth of theatrical styles, and met theatre-lovers and theatre-creators all across the country, some of whom I have since collaborated with artistically.

But most importantly, I learned how to write.

Cassandra, as it exists now, is quite different from the text presented on opening night. Performing one's own work is a gift to an emerging playwright. I had the opportunity to figure out—in the line of fire—what was working, and what wasn't. Having that sort of access to an audience, and being forced to not only "sit through" but live through every moment of my first play, taught me an immense amount about writing. I made major structural changes in the days or weeks between festivals, taking into account my numerous mid-sentence onstage revelations: having x before y would really make moment z more poignant…

More specifically, I learned about writing comedy. If a joke didn't land, I had the luxury of trying the delivery six different ways before finally admitting it wasn't funny. I tried to put the writing first, allowing myself to die out there as a performer multiple times for the sake of a line. I assumed, having more training in writing than acting, that it must be the performer's fault, not the writer's. Sometimes this was true. Sometimes the line just needed to be cut.

Performing one's own work also presents a unique set of challenges: clearly delineating the writer's time from the actor's time is one example. As my frequent re-writing process would attest, I don't know whether that ever happened with *Cassandra*. The writer in me simply wouldn't quit. This became evident during the rehearsal process when the words START REHEARSING TODAY, which had been scrawled across my agenda for eight days straight, continued to be ignored. Each night, I had assured myself that the next day the script would be ready.

Standing backstage on our opening night in Ottawa, under-rehearsed and terrified, I distinctly remember having this thought: If they don't like the show, I am the reason. Of course this is an incredibly unhealthy attitude, but one that is easy to fall into when wearing so many hats simultaneously. It was with complete and total fear that I threw myself out on stage that first night and every night after for an entire summer. (Interestingly, this nudged me towards a life of pseudo-sadism, teaching me that the experiences which are initially most terrifying are in the end most rewarding.)

I will never understand anything I write as intimately as I do *Cassandra*, because stepping into that role before an audience, repeatedly, provided insight that I could not have gained in isolation.

Cassandra was written to be performed by, and for, adults. But from the very beginning, that was questioned. Throughout the tour I was approached by parents who wanted a copy to read to their children. Many educators insisted *Cassandra* should be presented in the school system. I was thrilled to meet a number of young audience members who, though often shy, seemed to have enjoyed the play...my favourite being a nine-year-old named Cassandra from Victoria, B.C. During the run of FemFest in Winnipeg, I performed twice in schools—one elementary, one high school —the latter seeming to have more resonance.

Later, a friend and past collaborator, Shannon Scott, who had seen the original production several times, approached me about directing her own version—one which would have twelve-year-old Ally Connelly playing the title role. Although it had never occurred to me that this was a possibility, I was immediately on board. And I think Cassandra would have been too! After all, she was fighting to be taken seriously. So why not trust someone that age with such a challenge?

This new production ran at the London Fringe Festival in 2010. So, years after writing the play, I watched a performance for the very first time. Not only was I allowed to laugh at my own jokes, but all the heartbreak I experienced while writing it rushed back in a new way. It seems to me more difficult to escape the sad realities Cassandra is experiencing in the hands of a younger performer.

Cassandra was conceived as a ten-minute performance for a class assignment in my last year at York University. We were asked to interview a member of our faculty, capture their essence, and write a piece inspired by them. I chose acting teacher and novelist David Rotenberg because he scared me more than anyone else at the school.

He was incredibly generous, and after spending an hour in his office, I was left to capture his "essence." What began in my head was a wrestling match between Rotenberg's pragmatism and the wide-eyed dreamer inside me. My way of combating his realist worldview was by thrusting it into a less obvious place: the body of a nine-year-old girl. After Rotenberg viewed that initial ten-minute piece, his comment was "she got me."

When I began to expand the piece, the thematic struggle continued. Eventually, I learned with the help of my dramaturg, Kim Sider, that this ongoing battle was actually the central conflict of the play, not just a fight in my head. And as such, it could be voiced and explored throughout the piece, rather than having to come to a decision before starting to write it.

The message of the play is simple, and one that's been told time and time again. But I think what makes Cassandra unique is that we are required to watch her struggle with these opposing forces and come to terms with them. Not only is she brave enough to recognise the reality of her circumstances, but she moves boldly forward in an effort to change them. My favourite piece of press on the tour was from Bill Stuart of *Monday Magazine*: "Cassandra should be embraced as a wise-beyond-her-years role model for us all."

I like imagining a world where Cassandra, unlike her Trojan namesake, will find an audience with whom to share her wisdom.

Dianne & Me

by Ron Fromstein

Characters

EMMA — a fifteen-year-old girl

Production History

Dianne & Me is most closely associated with one actress, Elena Juatco. She workshopped the show in Prescott, then debuted it at the Vancouver International Fringe Festival (2011).

From there it has gone on to be performed in Stratford (at the Springworks Arts festival), for Angelwalk Theatre (in Toronto), and at the Staircase Theatre (Hamilton). Our director has been Luke Brown, and the company name is My Lucky Penny Productions.

Dianne & Me was the winner of the 2009 Canadian National Playwriting Competition, the Ottawa Little Theatre playwriting Competition and the 2010 Hamilton Fringe New Play Competition.

ACTRESS — Elena Juatco
DIRECTOR — Luke Brown

This earlier version of the show opened at the 2010 Hamilton Fringe Festival. It was performed by Taryn Jorgensen, directed by Jaclyn Scoger and won best of Fringe.

Lights up on a young woman, centre.

EMMA: It's not true that we're all like our mothers.

It's not and I'm not.

(emphatic) I am not like my mother.

I mean, we're similar, sure, of course, she's my mom. I'm her daughter, I came from her—but we're not *alike*. And no, they're not the same.

Pause.

I sometimes hear her voice so clearly, I can't tell if she's there or not.

Like, one day, we're in gym — the boys have basketball practise on one side, we have volleyball on the other — when I hear it, my mother, that is — *"Careful, Emma."*

And then he's there. Brian. Brian Wolster. Tall. Tall even for tall, hair long and shaggy.

"How's practice goin'?"

"Good, thanks. You?"

"Good... Real good. Um, look... Can I maybe call you sometime?...Emma?"

"Yes."

"Can I?"

"You — you want to call me?"

And the girls — every girl, every single girl — is looking, watching.

And a spotlight shines down.

"Uhuh."

"Okay...sure."

"Cool."

I took from that that he was going to call — sometime that weekend — and then we were going to...you know...do something...of some sort...at some point...together.

Coffee.

Go to Commercial.

Something.

So I'm at home on Friday.

Nothing. Just…nothing.

Saturday.

The same.

Then it's Sunday:

Seven…

Seven thirty…

> *A phone rings.*

"Hey, Cin…no…I mean, not yet…yes…I will! I solemnly, solemnly swear to…"

(loud) "Emma."

(in kind) "Yeah?"

"Dinner's still ready."

"I — I'm not hungry."

"You'll be hungry later."

"Then I'll have something later."

"Well, come down and sit with me, then."

"Gotta go…you too."

> *She does.*

"So…"

"What?"

"How's your day? Emma?"

"Yes… What?"

"Go ahead."

"What'd I do?"

"You can go up if you like."

> *And she does.*

Nine…Nine-fifteen.

"Dinner's in the fridge."

"Thanks, Mom."

(quieter) Ten…ten o' four…five…

Nothing.

No missed calls.

No texts.

Not — "Hey, Em, couldn't… Sorry — Family thing. Practice. Super spent. Broke a limb. Broke several. Am typing this with my only remaining digit. Another time maybe?"

Just…nothing.

At no point do I get contacted by him in any—

"Emma."

"Yeah."

"Can I come in?"

"I'm in bed."

"Something you want to — "

"Goodnight, Mother."

And then I'm at school — Brenner Secondary, just off Arbutus — skaters are taking their last rides down the rails, bikes are being dismounted, locked up and run from in one fluid motion, teachers are at the second-floor windows looking out, and stoners are coming in like zombies from all known directions.

And I'm at my locker, getting ready, like you do.

Then he — Brian — comes along with a buddy of his, Kyle.

Kyle is a lot shorter and often, quite often, at his side, or around him.

"Hey, Emma."

And he's looking at me like nothing happened.

"You didn't call."

Kyle jets.

"What?"

"You…didn't…call."

And he sees my look.

This— You said you were going to and then you didn't. Do you know what happens if everyone who says they were—are—going to do something—doesn't?

"Uh…"

And goes. (back a step)

So I go. (forward)

It stops. The whole world stops.

"It does?"

Yes, it does. Absolutely. It absolutely and completely does.

Bananas get delivered brown—not green.

Jets slam into each other.

And their parts rain down, morning, day, and night.

It may sound dramatic, but that's what he's suggesting.

What men are saying when they say they will and then they don't.

(the voice again) "What'd I tell you?"

"So, uh…should I call you later?…Emma?"

Then I'm at home and we're— my mom, Dianne, and I — are eating pizza, extra…everything.

"So practice was okay?"

"Uhuh."

"And bio?"

"Fine."

"Anything else happen?"

Then she sees it — she sees something. Looks at me like — like I'm trapped in the centre — the exact centre point — of a massive forest fire.

And she's in a helicopter overhead with a rope.

"Did I ever tell you about — "

"Mother."

"Yes, Em?"

"Thank you very much for dinner."

She thinks that you just shouldn't trust them at all.

Boys, I mean.

Men.

That all they want is to put their hands, their bodies…there.

You know.

There.

She doesn't say the word, though.

She's going to be forty soon — soonish — and she doesn't say the word.

(*quiet, as her mom*) Vagina.

(*as herself*) Va-gi-na.

◆

A couple nights go by.

I'm at home, studying, when:

The phone rings. She regards it. It rings again. A deep breath or two.

"Hi."

"Hey…it's, uh, me."

"Uhuh."

"Can — can we hang out?…Emma?"

"When?"

"What are you up to now?"

So we do.

We go for a walk along English Bay.

I know — everybody walks there, hangs there, does stuff there, but it doesn't make it any less nice of a place to be.

We share fries. That is, he buys, I eat.

And we talk…walk…walk…talk…

And a few nights later, the same. Ice cream this time.

Then it's getting dark, so he walks me back.

And we're at my house, just in front.

And the crickets sound very loud suddenly.

So we go in, I get a Coke for me, milk for Brian, and we end up on the couch.

You know?

The couch.

And his hand touches mine as I give it to him. The milk, I mean.

He looks at me.

I look back.

"You have…" (gesturing milk-stache)

And I wipe it.

Like this. *(enact)*

He's got these soft little hairs on the top of his lip.

And we…*(kiss)* softly.

And again…for a while.

And pretty soon his, well, his — his male part, his maleness, his little Brian, is rubbing against me.

It wasn't out.

That would make it weird.

Which it wasn't.

It was…sorta nice.

Not like…coming home and the moment — the exact moment you enter the door, it starts raining, thundering after you, nice.

But nice all the same.

And he's rubbing and rubbing and —

"This is cool?"

"What?"

"This. It's okay?"

"Yeah…"

"For sure?"

"Yes…yes, for sure."

"Cool."

And we — Brian Wolster and I — kiss — are kissing again.

And now — now it's like he's on a mission.

Like Coach Jenkins pulled him aside at yesterday's game:

"You rubbed against any girls lately, Wolster?"

"Pardon, coach?"

"Of late, have you rubbed against any Brenner girls?"

"No, sir."

"No? No? Well, get out there…get out there, Wolster…get out and get rubbing… and don't come back—don't you dare come back until—"

And he's looking at me like "I'm rubbin' against you. I, Brian, am rubbing against you, Emma. What do you think about that, huh?"

Like I didn't notice.

Like I thought that that was his way of asking where the washroom was or something. Like I —

And then, then he well, he made this face…*(does it)*

And this sound *(does it)*

And his right leg shook.

It actually *(enacts)*

Like—like a frog's leg when the electric current runs through it.

You know?

It…just…when the door opens.

Wide.

Like in a western, when someone new enters the saloon.

And my mom is there.

Like she'd been waiting.

Like she'd been on the other side.

I'm not saying she had, it just seemed that way.

She's in her fancy clothes — white blouse, thin gold necklace, and she looks, well, pretty.

She's very pretty, my mom.

And Brian's face is like …*(enacts)*

And my mom is like…*(enacts)*

And I — I am…stuck…I am quite, quite stuck.

And could it be any more awkward?

Then this sandy-haired man in a navy blazer, no tie, came in behind her.

This "friend" of hers.

Paul.

And my mother turns to him, to Paul, and says, she says very calmly — "I'll call you later."

And he looks at me like — well, like "Good luck, kid."

And the wind slams the door hard behind him.

Or my mom did it with her mind.

Then she — Dianne — walks around, over to us.

Rain starts up again outside.

(gently) "Brian…"

I go to push him off me, only, only he's completely and absolutely still.

Not blinking even. *(enacts)*

(very quiet) "Brian."

His face and eyes follow her, but he's not moving.

"Brian."

And then she's this *(gestures)* close to us.

Him.

It.

And she saw.

She…saw.

And I could see she saw.

And she could see me seeing.

And time fully froze for a minute.

It just…stopped.

Like the gatekeeper of the universe pressed *hold on a sec* on his stopwatch.

Then she took a breath, walked around again and opened the door and looked at him the way drill sergeants do privates. *(does it)* And kept looking at him until he — in one full motion — rose up and walked to it and past it as sure as he had a tail and it was between his legs.

And the door slammed like to say "Get outta here, Brian Wolster, and take that thing a' yours, that crazy thing, with you. It's an animal. You're an animal. You're all animals."

Then she just stood there — not looking at me or anything — just breathing.

"Mom…Mom."

Nothing.

"Mom…Mother?" You said you'd be back late and we — we just…it just… Eight-thirty is not late. Eight-thirty is…eight-thirty."

She walks off, to her room, paces, then makes a call.

"Hi, Cin…yes, I did…interesting, it went very —"

When a note comes under the door "If you want to talk, I'm here."

(through the door) "Just a sec, Cin — I'm on the phone."

"Call her back."

"I'm talking with her now…sorry, Cin."

"We should talk, Emma."

"We?…We? Please, please go away."

"Five minutes."

"Go...away."

And I can feel her there, still.

Just...you know...being.

We don't talk because there's nothing—nothing—to talk about.

A boy I invited in came in.

We...we did what — what you do sometimes. That's what people do.

And seeing as how there's like, six billion of us, a lot of people — a lot — have done plenty more several times over.

    Somewhat calmed.

Around two, I come out to make myself a — but there's already one there — turkey, crusts cut off. Mayo on one side. Salad, dressing on the side.

And I watch TV really quiet.

(quiet) Like so you can barely hear what they're —

I think...I'm not sure...I'm not positive or anything, but I think I — I may have heard, I don't know, possibly, crying, from her room.

So I go to her door, and I — I didn't.

I wanted to but I — I just, well, I went to bed like you do, sometimes.

Only I'm not sleeping either.

You know.

Like when someone yawns, you yawn.

You know?

And then, sometimes you just *(re: getting emotional)...* It doesn't mean anything.

It's like — it's like when boys get...you know...what they get...there...you know...

They just...do.

If you could announce on a microphone to a massive speaker system that the world — the whole world — is going to end in five minutes...that some giant asteroid from some unknown galaxy is hurtling toward earth, and that its collision would cause a massive tidal wave, earthquakes, and general chaos, somewhere, some boy, no, no — hundreds, thousands, millions, armies of boys of all religions, countries and cities, would have them and look down at themselves and go "What is wrong with me? What is wrong here?"

It doesn't mean — they're pro end of the world.

It doesn't mean anything.

Other than the fact they're boys.

Kissing means something though.

It does.

It really does.

It's nice to be kissed. It is.

And it's nice to kiss back.

To kiss and be kissed.

And to kiss back more after being kissed like, "please, kiss me more, please, please, I'm enjoying this. I'm really really enjoying this. I like kissing."

All that's wrong with the world—and there's a lot—goes away when you're being kissed.

You could fix the whole Middle East thing with kissing.

And if it doesn't, if it doesn't at all make things better, even just for a moment, or a moment in a moment in a moment, this little starburst of a moment, you're not doing it right.

Or you're not doing it right for that person.

Or you weren't made to kiss each other.

Or be with each other at that moment.

That happens sometimes.

*

Then it's morning and there's berries, yogurt, and nuts in front of me.

"*You sure you don't want the rest?*"

"*Yes, thanks.*"

"*You're positive.*"

"*Uhuh.*"

"*Want a lift to school?*"

"*I said I'm— Sure.*"

And we're driving up Arbutus in the rain.

And the windshield wipers are trying to catch up.

But you can't. You can't catch up.

And my mom's leaning forward like this. *(does it)*

I put on the radio.

And it slows down a little.

> *She leans back.*

(singing) "*Guys you know you better watch out. Some —* "

She turns it off right away. Then drops it —

"*Do you want to hear about my first time? …Emma?*"

"*What?*"

"*Would you like to hear about, well, the first boy I was with?*"

"*I'll be late.*"

"*We've got fifteen minutes.*"

(singing) Some guys, some guys are only about

"*Em?*"

"*I've already been late this week.*"

"*I'll write a note.*"

"*A note?*"

"*Yes.*"

"*What? 'Dear Mr. Henderson: Sorry I've kept Emma away. It's just that, well, I'd begun to tell her about the first time I was with someone…you know… sexually — and wanted to finish.'*"

"*Emma?*"

"*What, Mother!*"

And she gets — it gets quiet.

The rain is bulleting down.

And now I'm imagining it:

A tuxed-up, white-gloved, smilin' George Clooney dancing…with my mother.

Hugh Jackman — serious-faced, blue jeans, white tank, grabbing her — my mother — with his metallic claw —

I'm not saying she shouldn't be with someone.

I'm not.

Only that she shouldn't talk about it — at all, whatsoever — to me.

"Em...Emma?"

(singing again) "That thing, that thing, that thhhiinngg. That..."

And she drops me off at the back, by the portables.

And doesn't go to hug me or anything.

Just looks at me and smiles.

And her eyes say "I love you so much," which is almost worse than actually saying it.

I don't say anything.

But I don't slam the door. I just kinda shut it.

◆

(Brian's voice) "Em...Hey, Emma."

Brian and I are there under the sheltered part, rain pattering just beyond us.

And he looks at me like "should I, uh, kiss you, or I won't if you don't want me to, I'll just — "

So I hug him.

And he hugs back. Holds me.

We're holding each other.

Close.

   School bell.

And he goes one way. I go the —

"Emma, Emma, Emma."

Cindy Wicklow. Hair red. Smoking.

"Girlfriend...mover and shaker...hustler and playa..."

"C'est moi."

"You should."

"What?"

(perhaps laughing) "What? What she says."

And she turns me around.

There's this poster of the basketball team, Brian in Front, Kyle and others behind, and the caption is — "Go team go."

And I have this…this vision of everyone in the gymnasium.

The whole school. But it's like tens of thousands.

A sea.

We're all sitting when a mike comes down from the ceiling like they do at boxing matches.

And Coach Jenkins takes the mike.

And it goes pin-drop quiet.

"I just want to say that Emma is thinking about getting with Brian Wolster."

And a cheer goes out from the crowd.

"And I think that's great. Just fantastic."

And they lose it. Everyone loses it.

And a spotlight comes on me. And Brian.

"Emma…Emma…E?"

"Yes."

"I would. And she would…and she…and he might…a little… But you, you Emma, you have an option that we do not."

"I do?"

"You do. I'm not telling you what to do or anything."

"Oh, no."

"I'm not. I'm just saying that…"

"Were you me…"

> *School bell.*

A mass of kids, stoned and otherwise, emerges from shrubs, cars, over fences, and speed past.

"So?"

"I'll see."

(much quieter) "Em-ma…Em-ma…Em."

♦

A day goes by.

Cindy and I go to the basketball game together.

Some school from North Van.

Brian hits basket after basket.

Like this. *(demonstrates)*

And this. *(demonstrates)*

Shoots free throw after free throw.

Waves as he runs down the court.

And everyone looks to see where he's waving.

Everyone.

I wave back.

Like you do.

The next day there's a volleyball match.

Brian is there with Kyle.

I block a shot, make a shot.

We rotate.

I wave.

He waves back.

(much quieter) "Em-ma…Em-ma…Em."

And then it's Friday, some of us have spares, some are already done for the day.

We're hanging out on the back lot.

Frisbees, hacky sacks.

When a drop comes and lands right here. Brian puts his jacket over me. Around me.

"Want to do something?"

"What?"

"I don't know."

So…we start walking.

And it comes a little more.

So we hide by a tree.

It stops.

We run.

Then it starts again.

And we're running to and from shelter.

Then just plain running.

Past the point where it matters how much you're splashing.

How wet everything is.

Then all the houses have gotten bigger and have double garages and we're going in the side entrance of one, going down the stairs, taking off our shoes.

Socks.

And a cat is there to greet us at the bottom.

This all-black cat named Linus.

And we pat him.

He — Brian — pats.

I pat.

Our hands meet.

And he — Brian — pats my hand — here.

And I pat back.

"Are your pants wet?"

"What?"

"Are the bottom of your pants still wet?"

"Oh."

They are.

So he says , "Should we, uh, put them in the dryer?"

And he looks at me.

Like this, (enacts) he looks at me.

And I look at him. Like this: (roughly the same)

Then he takes his off.

Just…off.

And he's there in his underwear.

His white, white underwear.

And you can — if you were looking, if you were noticing — you could see the outline of…

And he sees me looking.

And I see him seeing.

And it sits there a moment.

"When are your parents coming home, Brian?"

"They're out for dinner."

"And your sister?"

"Tofino."

(quiet) "Okay."

(in kind) "Okay."

So I take…mine off.

And I'm there…in my…my (noticing) faded pink panties with a rainbow on them in the centre— Shit.

And he smiles but he doesn't laugh.

Just puts our clothes in the dryer.

And the universe is very much on hold and very much alive.

"Wanna see my room?"

And he takes my hand.

And we walk.

And he opens the door, turns the light on partway.

A large poster of Michael Jordan is on one wall, Kobe Bryant on the other, above there's glow-in-the-dark stickers, and on the other wall there's a corkboard with pictures of Brian skiing, playing ball, as a baby — he's kissing my neck really slow.

Then we're on his bed.

And he — he's looking at me. He's got this really goofy face, y'know, "Hey... you know whose bed you're on?...mine...you are on my bed...and you know who's there with you?...me."

Then we're...well...he's...I'm...we're just in our underwear...then not so much.

And he says, what he actually says is *"Wow, Emma...just...wow."*

What I say is — "I haven't before."

And what he says back, so quiet I'm not sure I heard it or not: "Me neither."

And I say "I'd like to be — "

And he takes out a package from the stand beside the bed. An unopened box.

And we start to — to really kiss. You know?

"Brian."

"Yeah."

"You have to open it."

"Right...right."

Then he's opening it...it's on...my eyes are shut...and then he's...well... there...you know...there...he...he's done.

"Shit."

"What? What?"

"Brian...Brian!"

He moves out and I'm like — "Oh, my God…oh, my God."

Then I'm in the washroom washing.

I'm washing and I'm rinsing and I'm rinsing and I'm washing.

When I get back, he's sitting there like we've just killed somebody and have to figure out what to do with the body.

    Buzzer sound.

The dryer.

My pants are on and I'm off.

"Hi, Cin…it's me…I went to Brian's…I went…we…call…please."

Ten seconds after I'm in the door, a car pulls up.

    Deep breaths.

"Hi, Emma…"

"Hi."

"What?"

"Nothing."

"Emma…"

"I'll be upstairs."

"Emma…Em."

And a note comes under the door almost before it's shut.

And a text from Cin —"At gig. Will call later. Way to go!"

◆

Monday comes around somehow. Brian comes up to me after school.

"I, uh…wanted to say , about, uh, the other day…"

"Yes…"

"I…well…I…"

And it doesn't come out.

I don't know if I shut it in with my eyes or it gets stuck somewhere in him but it doesn't come out.

And we don't talk about it after.

We just…don't.

We say hi, we wave. I sometimes find myself looking at, or being looked at, but we don't talk.

Then I'm in Henderson's morning bio when—*(hand up)* "Washroom, please."

    Nausea.

Cindy is there, like, a moment after me. Holds my hair.

Pours water into those little dixie cups.

She's giving me this look I haven't seen before. This completely new look.

"What?…What?…You're freaking me out."

"After school, by the portables."

From there we walk for, like, forever.

Down Arbutus.

To Burrard.

Across the bridge.

Then we're in a drugstore…getting a — a pregnancy test.

And she puts it in my purse.

"I should get going home."

"I'll come with."

"I'll call you."

And she looks at me. That same look.

"I'll call."

But I don't.

Instead, I give it another week.

Some girls — a lot of girls — are irregular.

And even if you're not regularly irregular you could be sometimes, you could.

You easily, easily could.

Stress…sports…a lot of things can affect it. Things.

So I give it time…space.

But nothing.

Just…nothing

Then it's Saturday, my mom's in the shower and I—I take it.

Two blue lines come.

Which means…well…

My mom comes out. Is putting on makeup. I help.

"What's up, Emma?"

"Nothing."

"Nothing at all?"

"Nope."

We put on foundation, rouge.

She has on these click-clacking heels and this great red blouse and skirt.

"You look very nice."

"Thank you…"

"I like how your—"

"Emma. Is there something you'd like to talk about?"

"I'm okay."

And she looks at me a minute.

Cups my chin.

The doorbell goes.

"We can talk later."

"We're talking now."

And the doorbell goes again. My mother opens the window. Paul is down below, looking more like a teenage boy than I've ever seen a grown man look.

"I can't go out tonight. I'll call you later."

But he's still there.

So she says it again.

"I'll call you…later."

And he looks back for a moment and then is like "Well, all right then."

Then we're in the kitchen, sipping mint tea. She's not saying anything. Not asking. We're just…there.

"I was…Brian and I, we…we…"

And she puts her hand on mine. But it won't come out like words.

"We — we just…we were…"

And she just combs my hair with her hands.

And I — I show her the box and she — she just swallows and breathes. I can feel her breathing.

And she says, she says *"Okay…it's okay, Emma…everything is okay."*

Like it wasn't a biggie. It was just…another thing…like leaving a little bit of milk in the fridge and not throwing it out.

When I go to bed, I hear someone at the door and I go to the top of the stairs and Paul is there holding her as she — as she tries to get it out.

And then she is…she's…convulsing, like someone is stabbing her with a knife.

Repeatedly.

And after he goes, she is down there again.

Alone.

Phone in hand.

I go to—to say something, but words don't come.

So I—I don't.

I just don't.

◆

In the morning we're in her doctor's office, who is very to the point.

"You're pregnant, Emma. About eight weeks."

My mother squeezes my hand.

"Do you have any questions?"

"No."

"Do you want to talk to me alone for a moment?"

"No."

"You can if you want to."

"That's okay…thanks."

Then she—the doctor—takes off her glasses and says, she just says it— *"What do you want to do?"*

Like she's asking me if I want the chicken or the fish.

"We'll talk about it."

And we leave.

Outside, there's no cloud or rain whatsoever. It's a disturbingly beautiful and perfect day.

Birds fly in V formation.

We get all green lights.

In our driveway my mother says:

"Do you want to take time off school?"

And I hear me say *"Okay."*

So I take a day.

Which becomes two.

Then three.

I knock on my mom's door one night.

"Just so you know, I don't want to talk about other options."

And I look at her.

And she looks back.

"Okay…all right."

Then it's the weekend.

And Monday.

Brian isn't at school.

Kyle comes up to me straightaway.

"Brian wants you to know…he's sorry."

"Okay."

When I get home, there's a car other than my mother's in the driveway.

Brian's parents.

Mrs. Wolster looks at me and looks at me like—like I swooped down from the sky, grabbed him—Brian—took him to a mountaintop lair, climbed up on him and made him.

Mr. Wolster doesn't say much. He looks just like Brian, with lines in his forehead, gray at the side of his temples, and he looks anywhere but at me.

Brian isn't there.

"Do you want to stay out here?"

"Is that okay?"

So she makes tea.

Goes in with them.

◆

At school, it's…well, it's out.

Like it's a tangible thing almost.

The looks.

The non-looks.

The strange hellos.

Cindy's cool with me, though. She walks with her arm around me down the second-floor hall, the one that seems to go on for, like, ten miles.

"Look until they look away…blow a kiss…now while rubbing your belly…add some tongue…We could say it's from a donor of our choosing."

And she smiles.

Her hair is now bright green.

Every day my mom's car is at the back, by the portables.

And, well, it goes how it goes.

Weeks go by.

The semester ends.

Over the holidays, everyone skis and snowboards.

Cindy's doing shows on the island.

Me, I'm in my room a lot, crying…studying…vomiting…crying…when this knock comes, really softly at the door.

"Come in."

And she, my mom, Dianne, comes in and sits at the side of my bed.

"Do you want to move?"

"Where?"

"There's a branch office in Toronto."

And I look at her for a moment.

And she holds it.

"Now?"

"When you like."

"When I like."

"Yes."

Then she goes.

And well, we do.

I mean, we talk about it, we work it out with the school. My mom's on the phone and computer to Toronto, but it gets worked out.

Paul drives us to the airport and then we're on a plane. In the air. Approaching the Rockies.

Over the Rockies. Then…pretty soon…the 401…still on the 401…a little more still…a little more after.

We go to my grandmother's, just west of the Annex. It's a three-level house with a long driveway and garage in back. Which we live on top of—my mom and me, that is.

I go to this alt school nearby.

Lots of independent work.

There are three other girls like me there.

Nobody suggests or says anything, but one afternoon we all end up eating at the same table in the caf and no matter how late one of us gets there, the table is always, always open.

We don't talk, we don't look at each other directly, we just sit there.

Part of me wants to say something though, like "Hey…I have something going on here too… Let's see: Jock…rain…yourself? Wanna go for lunch or ice cream or something?"

But I don't, 'cause, well…

I just go to school, eat, and pee a lot.

Basically.

That's what I do.

◆

"Mom. What are you doing tonight?"

"I…well, to be honest with you, some of the girls at —"

"I'm sorry. I'll just — "

"Emma."

"Uhuh."

"What would you like to do?"

"What would I like?"

"Yes."

So we go to the movies.

My…well, my mother and I.

On a Friday.

Rainbow Cinemas. On Front.

We get popcorn with lots of butter.

And I see kids — a few kids from school. We don't exactly talk but we do that thing you do when you see someone you know.

Hey…hey. (enact head thing)

And my mom just kinda…pulls back a bit, you know…takes in all the posters they have. "Oh, look at this movie with the aliens and zombies and zombie aliens."

And we sit in the third row, the whole time my mother leaning back, like *(enacts)*

After, we' re walking to the subway — they have fully underground subways in Toronto — but it's colder than it seems it should be.

"We can get a cab, if you like."

"What?"

"We can get a cab."

"Since when do we take cabs?"

"Since…well…sorry, Emma."

And I'd run off ahead, but first of all, I don't know my way around, and second, I can't.

"Hot chocolate, Em?"

"Sure."

So we do.

"I enjoy your company very much, Emma."

And she looks at me a moment…she looks at me…to make her point.

And I look back.

Then we're walking again. And on the subway.

At home, there's a note under the door that there's extra lemon pie in the main kitchen if we'd like.

I go. My mother does not.

After, I'm at her door with some tea, but she's asleep.

She sometimes falls asleep reading. Her face to the side, mouth like this. *(enacts)*

So I leave a note beside her. *"Thanks for tonight."*

And go to bed.

◆

Then it's Sunday and we do a square walk along Harbord up to and along Bloor, stop at Honest Ed's and get things we don't really need and take pleasure in how little they have cost us, then go back down to Harbord and home.

Wednesdays is new restaurant night.

There's Sushi on Bloor. Which is pretty good.

Utopia on College. Amazing burgers. I am a woman who enjoys burgers of late.

Fresh on Spadina. Best sweet potato fries ever.

We're there one day, one night when —

"Emma, Paul was thinking of coming out and I was wondering if that would be —"

"That's fine."

"You're sure?"

"Yes."

"It doesn't have to be. If it bothers you in any way —"

"Mom."

"Yes."

And I look at her.

Take the rest of her fries.

Next weekend, Paul comes out.

He stays at a hotel on Bloor near Spadina. She spends a long time getting ready.

"How do I look?"

"Fantastic."

"You're not just saying that?"

"Do I ever pay you false compliments?"

And we look at each other…through the mirror.

"You're sure it's okay if I —"

"Go."

"You'd say if you needed me to —"

"Go, Mother. Go out. Go."

And when she goes, I am still looking at the mirror.

A fat woman is looking back at me.

She's huge.

Like it's a circus mirror…only it's not.

I am still looking when she comes back. She runs in crying.

"Mom…Mom."

"It's nothing…I'm fine."

"Talk."

"It's fine."

"It's not. Speak. Speak to me."

And she looks at me. And I look back.

"Paul and I may not be — "

And right away, like he'd been waiting, there's a knock at the door.

"Hi, Emma, I just wanted to tell your mom I — "

"No…"

"Pardon me?"

"No, you can't talk to her right now."

"Excuse me?"

"You can't."

"If you could just — "

"You can't talk to my mother right now."

And I shut the door slowly and firmly.

And my mother is looking at me.

"What? What?"

◆

In the morning, she's not up, so I make some scrambled eggs.

And at night, I make a stirfry.

And for the next few days I wake her.

Help pick outfits.

And bring her tea most — *"Mom!"*

"I'm here…what…sit…what?"

"Something."

And she puts her hand here. And it —

"Kick."

"What?"

"It's kicking."

"Kicking."

And she nods.

And when I come out of the washroom that night my mother is waiting there.

"Do you need help getting into bed?"

"I — sure."

And she does.

She helps me get down.

And comfortable.

And tucks me in.

Puts her hand here.

"Wake me if you need to."

"Okay."

"You promise?"

"I…" She is looking at me very closely. *"I promise."*

◆

One day my grandmother announces she's going out of town for a few days.

No big goodbye.

The very next day, it's dark outside.

In the day.

There's been, there is a complete and absolute power failure.

Luckily, AA batteries were on sale last week at Honest Ed's. So we bought 128 of them.

And she — Dianne — reads to me.

And I read back.

And it goes a second day.

A third.

Fourth.

Four days.

So we barbecue up all the meat in the freezer.

Sit by the window.

Play cards. We play — *"Mooommmmm."*

"I'm here...I'm here...just a minute, Emma..."

And she goes out to start the car...only our car is in Kitsilano.

And she comes back — *"We don't have a car here, Emma."*

"No, we don't."

She calls for a cab, but they don't pick up.

Then she calls 911.

"Yes...yes...what do you mean how deep into labour is she? She's in labour... yes, this is her first child...you're putting me on hold? Emma!"

An ambulance, we're told, will be on the way shortly...though an exact time can't be given.

You are not in any immediate danger and so they will not be here just yet.

"But they are coming."

"Yes. Yes, they are. It's fine...it is...we're all right...we're good."

Only it's not...we're not.

And we breathe. And we — *(breathing)*

And Coach Jenkins is there across from me — "That's a Wolster you got in there. A likely starting forward or centre for Brenner. You will deliver this child healthy, Emma. You will deliver it. I will train it. It will one day play for —"

We breathe. And breathe. *(enact)*

She wipes my forehead.

She elevates my head.

Helps me off with my — my pants.

And a while goes by.

A good while.

And then…

    Siren sound.

And the whole street is there, watching me go in.

And I'm on a stretcher.

In the back.

And they have chosen the bumpiest sidestreet route possible.

Then I'm at the Women's Hospital on Gerrard.

In a room.

And…and…pretty soon, not immediately after, but soon I…I —

"It's okay…it's okay…"

    Breathes.

"Doin' good…doin' great…"

A — something is coming out of my body.

From me.

From my —

There is a head…body…arms…tiny, little squirmy hands…feet…

A — a child has come out of me.

This…little girl.

With…five…ten fingers…ten toes.

A nose…eyes…two…

This beautiful little six-pound, ten-ounce girl.

Christina.

Christy.

And she's there — my mother is there — when I get up and when I go to sleep.

On the same chair.

There are very large black bags beneath each of her eyes.

And she looks — well, not like she usually looks.

"How are you feeling?"

One of the nurses.

"Good."

"Someone has talked to you about feeding?"

"Yes."

"Good."

"Get out."

They don't say that, but at the same time it's not all that different than eating at a busy Chinese restaurant around Chinatown. "Hi, what can we get you? Here it is, enjoy, can I take this away for you?…how was it?…good…get out. Go."

So we do.

We go to my grandmother's.

We sit in the main house living room. Christina cries. I feed her.

My mom drinks tea. I nap. Christina cries. I wake up.

And that becomes…normal…ish.

As does getting up at two…four…five…or not, napping at noon, and sleeping, trying to sleep, by nine. Nine pm. Every night.

For a while.

And we — Dianne & I — sit on gorgeous patios with rush-hour traffic in front.

Walk along Harbourfront, with Christy.

And we just…sorta — you know — hang out.

Like you do.

And somewhat warm weeks go by like they do from time to time in Toronto.

And time goes amazingly fast and incredibly slow.

And then one day, I'm there with Christina, and my mother is reading the *Vancouver Province*, and a book by Douglas Coupland and listening to Sarah McLachlan.

"Do you want to go home?"

"What?"

"Do you want to go home, Mom?"

And she nods.

She makes calls and is on the computer and three-and-a-half weeks later we're back in Kits.

And it's raining.

This great, soft, wonderful rain.

And the wipers are trying to catch up.

And catch up.

And Cindy calls, comes over. Her hair is now…brown, like her eyebrows, and she's not smoking.

And Brian's parents have called.

And come over.

With a blanket that says Christy on it.

"Hello, Emma."

"Hi, Mrs. Wolster."

"How are you?"

"Fine…thank you. You?"

And she reaches out her arms and I pass Christy over.

And she looks over at the car. And Brian comes out. He is wearing jeans with no rips and a cardigan.

His hair is short.

"Hi."

"Hey."

They start coming over once a week, on Sundays. And Mrs. Wolster calls me dear and makes a point of hugging me every time she sees me and holding me until I pull back a bit.

And then it's school.

Takes a breath.

And I put on one dress.

"No."

And then another.

"Maybe."

And another.

"Yes…yes."

And breastfeed Christina.

And pump some milk out.

And my mom knocks on the door and says *"Do you want a ride?"*

"Sure."

And we get to school, and my mother goes *(mouthing)* "I love you."

And I go, I say, *"I love you, Mom."*

'Cause she's my mother.

And, well…you know…I do.

I do.

> *Lights go down.*

About the playwright

Ron Fromstein is a largely self-taught playwright from Toronto. He is a three-time winner of the Canadian National Playwriting Competition (2006, 2007, and 2009) and six-time winner-finalist of the Toronto Fringe 24 hour playwriting competition. Other works include *Just Us, The Big Smoke,* and *One in a Million* (a micromusical).

For more info — www.ronfromstein.com

Interview

The first thing for me is: How much do I care about the central character? I say this as I tend to have several works on the go and invariably lose interest in some. I don't mean to, but I do. Others, like Emma in *Dianne & Me*, seem to stick, to take on a life of their own that goes well beyond the original concept. I try my best to allow for and be open to that. To give the story and the character(s) space to live and breathe, like people everywhere want to have. With *Dianne & Me*, the monologue itself came out fairly fast. So I started sending it out to various contests using the deadlines to help me complete draft after draft.

From there, *Dianne & Me* was fortunate enough to receive several awards and each brought with it some fantastic workshopping opportunities. In BC, where it won the Canadian National Playwriting Competition, Janet Michael helped dramaturge (I had worked with her before so we have a sort of shorthand) and Emma Wong was the actress. Janet asks great questions. She's very clear that she's not always looking for or wanting an immediate answer, just that she has a question about a particular moment or scene, and that if it helps me out in some way, great.

As to Emma (the actor), we were very pleased that she was both close to the age of the character and quite open to talking about what parts of the script struck particularly true for her and what parts did not. With Janet helping to facilitate, I feel like we hit the ground running.

The same process occurred in Ottawa (where it won a separate award), though we had less time there and I didn't know everyone quite so well. From there, it was on to the Fringe. I didn't do many changes (beyond the previous workshops) with Taryn and Jackie in the first Fringe production for reasons mostly of time.

After our Fringe/Best of Fringe run, I was approached by Luke Brown & Theatre Aquarius about the piece. Luke had some very good questions about the character(s) and the piece in general. We connected fairly fast. The process then became meeting up with our new actress Elena Juatco and Luke Brown once a month in Elena's Toronto kitchen-living room and working it through, over and over, until we felt it was a much improved and streamlined show.

Elena's emotional honesty was very helpful here. Some things connected intuitively for her. Some things did not. Questions were asked. Once again, instead of trying to answer reflexively, I tried to breathe them in and let them affect me and the script. Working with the same performer for an extended period was great for me. We all got to be meaningfully involved in the growth and discoveries of the character(s) and the show, I feel, positively reflected that.

We then started touring it: Vancouver Fringe, a festival in Stratford, Prescott, Hamilton again, Toronto.

The joy for me now, as both a playwright and person, is seeing how much fun Elena is having with the show. When we do a performance, her question is inevitably: Where to next? When and how can we do it again? The emotional reaction of the people that approach Elena post-show is amazing. People seem to be sincerely moved and touched. Which is great for us, as both artists and people.

Back to the writing: Secondary characters were and continue to be a concern. Are they justified within the narrative or are we being showy in including them? To cut to it: does the audience need to meet them and get to know them or should they just be for us, the creative team? I feel this is often problematic in one-person shows. With *Dianne & Me*, I'm pretty happy with who, beyond Emma (our protagontist) and Dianne (the mom/antagonist), we get to meaningfully know. Her best friend, her boyfriend, her coach, and a few others. Secondary characters populate Emma's world but they are not the focus of the show. The show is called *Dianne & Me*. That's who we promised the audience and ourselves we'd tell a story about. And that's what I think we do.

A related concern continues to be: What in the story is absolutely necessary? *Dianne & Me* is a fifty- to sixty-minute, 7000-word monologue. Do we lose the audience anywhere? Anywhere at all? Even for a moment? I feel this needs to be asked over and over and over again. It's a great post-show question and helps keep a show/production honest.

The other major question I like to keep asking is: Does the show clip along at a healthy pace for both performer and audience? Does it breathe where it should breathe, gallop where it should gallop, and trot when it should trot? For me it does. I've seen it a bunch and hope to see it more, as each time I do I see or notice something, however small, I hadn't before.

Last thing: The current temptation is to keep on tweaking, adding a line here, cutting a line there. It's hard to just sit in the back of the theatre and enjoy what everyone else is enjoying: A single actor telling the story of her relationship with her mother, while gracefully inhabiting a half dozen or so other characters. There's a certain magic to it for me. On the one hand, a monologue is just a single person standing there talking to us. On the other, it's a complete world, an intimate world that we've made and are now letting audiences in on.

I'm very much in awe of what Elena and the other actors who've performed (and workshopped) the role are able to embody and inspire in fifty-five minutes on stage, alone.

All My Day Jobs

by Kirsten Van Ritzen

Characters

KIRSTY (F) — various ages

Production History

Victoria Fringe Festival (2011)
Regina Fringe Festival (2008)
Carousel Studio, Vancouver (2008)
Final Draught Play Reading Series, Vancouver (2007) excerpts

Credits for All Productions

ACTOR/PLAYWRIGHT: Kirsten Van Ritzen
DIRECTOR: Ian Ferguson
SOUND DESIGN: Alexander Brendan Ferguson
PRODUCED BY: Broad Theatrics

A stage is set with two tables that will transform into desks, counters, beds, cars. Three chairs upstage. A coat rack. Two boxes filled with props.

All characters played by one actress, with the exception of 3rd A.D. in Scene 16, which is best played live by a stage manager.

Scene 1: LECTURER #1

Actor enters, says hello to the audience. Puts on a lab coat and glasses. Speaks with a funny European accent.

LECTURER: What is a day job? One: a job that is not in your field. Two: a job that is of a temporary nature. Or so one hopes. Three: a job that does not make use of your education, training, God-given creativity or artistic vision. Usually a menial, low-paying, soul-sucking, brain-numbing job—in a customer service industry.

Who needs a day job and why? By definition, starving artists. Actors, singers, dancers, comedians, musicians, filmmakers, writers, sculptors. Poets. Anyone who is expected to do what they love for free. Forever. Even those artists who get paid and are considered "professional" still need a day job.

Fun fact: A day job may also be performed at night! What makes a perfect day job? One: free food. Two: paid in cash. Three: minimal humiliation. Four: co-workers who cover for your auditions. Five: a boss who is not asshole.

How to land a day job: Look good. Speak English. Lie like hell. Example: What is your availability? "Anytime." How long will you stick around? "Forever. I want this job until I die." Do you enjoy working with the public? *(long pause)* "Yes."

Lab coat and glasses removed.

Scene 2: DINER WAITRESS

Actor speaks as herself, the narrator.

KIRSTY (NARRATOR): My best friend Karen suggests we apply for jobs at Salisbury House—a chain of restaurants in Manitoba, currently owned by Burton Cummings. Think of a White Spot, only not so classy. Karen is large-boned—she's Ukrainian—but her hair feathers perfectly in a Pat Benatar haircut.

KAREN: Kirsty, we need more money for rollerskating. I'm tired of my paper route, and you're too old to babysit. The popular girls all own their own skates.

KIRSTY (NARRATOR): She's right. We are fifteen years old. We love to meet guys and we love roller disco. My dad drives us every Tuesday, right after my piano lesson. You have to pay the entry fee, the skate rental, pop, chips, a locker and four bucks to split a pack of smokes. Player's Light. I don't inhale.

KIRSTY: But, Karen, I don't know how to be a waitress. (*she takes a drag and coughs*)

KAREN: Don't worry, we'll just be clearing tables and stuff. My cousin says it's really easy.

> *SFX: restaurant noise.*

KIRSTY (NARRATOR): First day. Mustard-yellow polyester zip-front dress, pantyhose, black cotton mary-janes made in China. Karen isn't here. Or her cousin.

LARGE MALE CUSTOMER: Whatsa difference between the Big Nip and the Cheese Nip?

KIRSTY (NARRATOR): Sal's are famous for their burgers, which are called Nips. An Egg Nip is a burger with a fried egg on it. If "Nips" makes you think of the Japanese, you might be a World War Two veteran. If "Nips" make you think of mammaries, well, you're probably…a guy. Anyway.

KIRSTY: Um, a Big Nip has fried onions, I think. The Cheese Nip has cheese?

CUSTOMER: I hate onions. Gimme one without onions. No lettuce, no tomato. Bacon. Extra cheese. Side of fries. With gravy. And soup.

Kirsty: Is that … the Deluxe Cheese Nip Platter?

CUSTOMER: How should I know? Just bring it to me. And a diet Coke. Nah, make that a chocolate shake.

KIRSTY (NARRATOR): Super Nip, Deluxe Nip, Plate or Platter? They said to memorize the menu but I had to study for my French exam. And a milkshake? Goldarnit. Order on the wheel. Rich gives me a wink. White paper hat. Brown hair, brown eyes. Really cute! Really bad acne, but he is a line cook — I mean, standing over a deep-fryer can't be good for your skin.

KIRSTY (NARRATOR): Laura, the head waitress — five plates of wafer pie — all on her left arm:

LAURA: Hey, newbie… Did you make the last pot of coffee? Ya forgot to put in a filter… And do your side work — a tray of roll-ups and refill the ketchups.

KIRSTY: Um…how do you make a…shake?

KIRSTY (NARRATOR): Rich leans over the pass-through.

RICH: Two scoops of ice cream, big squirt of chocolate syrup, fill 'er up with milk and put it in the mixer.

> *He rings the bell—ding.*

KIRSTY: Thanks.

Makes shake, making flirty eye contact with Rich and giggling.

KIRSTY (NARRATOR): Laura is already back for an armload of platters.

LAURA: Hey, let's hustle, Tables twelve and thirteen are yours too...

KIRSTY: Okay, I'll...oh, oh, oh!

Milkshake spills all over her.

LAURA: Ya gotta HOLD it, clip doesn't work...

KIRSTY (NARRATOR): Now she tells me. My hand is going numb—the chocolate is dripping into my, oooh—I've got a run in my pantyhose—and an entire little league team just sat in my section—the tables are still dirty from the last customers— Did I even give them their bill? Maybe I can reach the soup while I'm here. *(tries to reach)* Hot hot hot—cold cold cold. *(switch hands)* Aaah. Cold cold cold—hot hot hot.

KIRSTY (NARRATOR): Rich rings the bell *(ding)*...and puts up my Cheese Nip Platter *(ding)* the Super Nip Plate *(ding)* and the Sail Boat of Fish Nips. I bet I could take these all at once, just like Laura!

Circus music underscores a juggling/spinning plates fantasy lazzi that ends with the SFX of crashing plates.

KIRSTY (NARRATOR): My best friend Karen and I bought white rollerskates and pink satin jackets—but we lost interest in the roller rink. We had boyfriends. Karen and Greg—another line cook—me and Richard. Rich was a smart guy—he was going to be a structural engineer—and also romantic—he wrote me love poems on paper napkins. Our first kiss was in the walk-in, pressed up against the frozen beef patties. Welcome to the work force.

Scene 3: ENUMERATOR-ELECTIONS CANADA

KIRSTY (NARRATOR): When an election is called, the government needs enumerators to go door to door to update the voter's list. They send me — middle-class white girl — to enumerate the residential hotels in the notorious red-light district. My mom's ancient Cadillac attracts the attention of several women I can only assume are prostitutes.

HOOKER: Hey, honey, you new here? No? Well, see ya.

KIRSTY: (reads building sign) "No knives allowed. No exceptions."

SFX: creaky, dripping.

KIRSTY (NARRATOR): Dark hallway. Dead rat. Dirty needle.

She timidly knocks, three times, then is about to skedaddle.

DRUNK GUY: Ged lost, I'm sleepin' in here.

KIRSTY: I'm here to enumerate you.

DRUNK: Like the sound of that. Lookee here, it's the Avon Lady. Come on in, I got beer.

KIRSTY: What's your name are you a Canadian citizen are you domiciled in this riding for the last six weeks?

DRUNK: Whoa there, sweetie, what're you sellin'... Girl Guide cookies? Lookee here, I got somethin' in my pants for ya...

KIRSTY: I gotta go.

DRUNK: Hey! I'se just showin' ya my ID! I'm a member of the Conservative Party—but now I'm thinkin' of votin' for the Liberals—I don't care for their fiscal policies no more!

SFX: car tires screeching.

Scene 4: TELEMARKETER - STATISTICS CANADA

She sits at a desk.

KIRSTY (NARRATOR): It's spring term of my first year in university. I haven't declared a major yet, but I'm thinking maybe psychology. My best friend Karen is finishing an accounting program at community college. We don't have time to hang out. I'm working evenings for Statistics Canada. Basically, I am a telemarketer on behalf of the federal government.

SFX: phone ring and pick-up click.

KIRSTY: *(reads in one breath)* Hello, this is Kirsty calling from Statistics Canada you have been randomly selected to participate in the annual Labour Force and Lifestyle survey this survey is being conducted across Canada and will be used to generate statistics that will affect transfer payments to various provincial departments such as education and health your identity and answers will remain confidential and you are legally compelled to participate. Is this a good time? *(listens, then replies)* Oh, it's easy. Age, gender, marital status. What is your annual income, have you ever been unemployed, did you spend your welfare cheque on luxuries like food, clothing or a parakeet? Stuff like that. *(listens)* Great! The survey will take approximately two hours and forty-five minutes to complete. *(listens, looks at her chest)* A blue shirt... oh, oh, ew!

She hangs up in disgust.

KIRSTY: *(disappointed)* Darn.

Scene 5: PERFUME SPRITZER

SFX: soft Muzak playing Christmas carols.

She stands in the cosmetics area of a major department store, holding a large bottle of perfume. She approaches shoppers with an offer to spritz their wrists.

KIRSTY: Passion? Passion? Passion?

She looks for more shoppers — and notices the front row of the audience.

KIRSTY: Would you like to try some Passion? Put some Passion in your life?

Ad libs with audience.

Goes back on stage. Sprays under her own armpit. Puts perfume on the counter. Checks watch. Bored to death, she saws her wrist, shoots her own head, hangs on a rope, finally drinks the bottle of perfume and dramatically "dies" on the floor. Stepped over by customers.

Scene 6: DANCING COCKTAIL WAITRESS

KIRSTY (NARRATOR): Third year of university — I'm a drama major with a minor in English — when opportunity knocks. A themed nightclub is opening up — it's "Happy Days Meets Grease" — and they need dancers. Not those kind. Clean, wholesome dancers who double as cocktail waitresses. We get cheerleader uniforms, and learn choreography to dozens of songs. When the club opens, the concept is a huge hit. I am promoted to Dance Captain right away, because I am one of the best dancers. I am also one of the worst waitresses.

SFX: crowd and music.

KIRSTY (NARRATOR): The place is packed with Yuppies doing the hand jive. I've got fourteen drinks over my head — ow *(guy steps on toe)* ow, and owww — cigarette burn — dammit. These dance tights cost sixteen bucks a pair! Maryth is waving at me from across the floor. If we don't do two numbers on the hour, every hour, the nightclub could lose its liquor licence. The DJ booth is shaped like a giant jukebox.

KIRSTY: Hey, Sheldon, let's do it — "Polka Dot" first and then it's "Shout."

KIRSTY (NARRATOR): "Itsy Bitsy Teeny Weeny Yellow Polka Dot Bikini" is a novelty song I have assigned to Loretta, a tall, gorgeous black girl.

LORETTA: You know I HATE this number.

KIRSTY: Sorry, Loretta, the other girls aren't ready. We need a solo.

KIRSTY (NARRATOR): She grabs the beach towel, and takes her spot in the middle of the dance floor. The rest of us have three minutes to deliver our drinks, grab our pompoms, and stand by. Allison is a pale redhead who once toured with Up With People.

ALLISON: *(grumpy and breathless)* There is so much smoke in here! I have asthma, you know. This number might make me pass out.

KIRSTY (NARRATOR): "Shout" is exhausting and at least ten minutes long. But the crowd always goes nuts.

> *SFX: song. She lip synchs and dances.*

> 'Weeeeell, you know you make me want to —
> shout—kick my heels up —
> shout—throw my hands up —
> shout—throw my head back,
> don't forget to say you will,
> don't forget to say ya ya ya ya'

KIRSTY (NARRATOR): Yes, I also lip-synch all the lead vocals. They are packed along the edges of the dance floor, singing and clapping along. They do the "little bit softer now" part right along with us, doing the twist right down to the floor.

> *Music: "little bit softer now, little bit softer now."*

KIRSTY (NARRATOR): Some guy with a moustache is staring at me and licking his lips—I think he's a hockey player. Here come the high kicks.

> *Music, kicks.*

KIRSTY (NARRATOR): Great, now he's staring at my crotch. And Allison just went down like a rag doll. Thunderous applause. Run, toss pompoms into DJ booth… arrgh—where is?…my float had two hundred bucks…got a blister on my toe and the burn hole is now a ladder running down my leg…and only five more hours to go.

Scene 7: DEPUTY RETURNING OFFICER - ELECTIONS CANADA

KIRSTY (NARRATOR): Elementary school gymnasium. Hand-painted banner: "believe it, achieve it!" It's Election Day, and I am a Deputy Returning Officer. All the other returning officers are senior citizens. Who else has nothing to do on a weekday? It will be a fourteen-hour shift, but at least I am sitting down, indoors, and no one is armed or drunk. I have packed two egg-salad sandwiches, one litre of diet Coke, and an amazing, inspirational book: *Acting is Believing*. Voters arrive. Check their ID, hand them a ballot. There is a big rush in the morning, then it gets real slow in the afternoon. I abandon my reading to converse with my co-worker, Edna.

EDNA (ELDERLY, KNITTING): My husband Ernie has gout. Would you like a fig? Church rummage sale is on Friday. I made thimble cookies. When my daughter Ellen was pregnant she had hemorrhoids something terrible. And gas. You look like her. Why aren't you in school today?

KIRSTY: I graduated last year. With a Bachelor of Arts degree.

EDNA: Oh, so you're a teacher then? How nice. I teach Sunday School every other week.

KIRSTY: No, I, um, I'm an actress. You know, in the theatre.

EDNA: I don't know why all the movies have so many curse words. Hollywood. It's just Sodom and Gomorrah. You should get married. My pastor has a nice-looking son. Would you like a fig?

KIRSTY (NARRATOR): Finally, it gets busy again and we are hopping until the polls close promptly at eight pm. I count the ballots in a precise and official manner, seal up the ballot box, then go home (sits and turns on TV with remote) and watch the returns come in from across the country. I feel like I am part of Democracy in Action.

> Realises she took the ballots home, slides the ballot box underneath her chair sheepishly.

Scene 8: CAFÉ WAITRESS

SFX: cash register ka-ching ka-ching.

NASAL CUSTOMER: Miss, these French fries are cold.

POMPOUS CUSTOMER: Miss, this sandwich isn't what I ordered.

TEENAGER: Miss, there isn't enough flavour in this milkshake — can you make it more vanilla?

FEMALE CUSTOMER SPEAKING VERY SLOWLY: Miss, what's better — this noodle bowl or that noodle bowl? I can't decide. Does this one have cilantro? I like cilantro, but not too much. Which one do you think is tastier?

KIRSTY (NARRATOR): I have no idea. The owners are so cheap the only food they let us eat for free is soup. I have seven other tables who all sat down at the same time because they work in the office tower next door and only get thirteen minutes for lunch. All my orders just came up, the fries are getting cold and the gravy is congealing as we speak…SO IF YOU COULD JUST PLEASE MAKE UP YOUR GODDAMNED MIND BEFORE I TEAR YOUR FUCKING HEAD OFF!

KIRSTY: (*smiling*) I recommend this one. It's delicious.

Scene 9: PUB WAITRESS

HOT GIRL: Miss, we are leaving. Can we get the bill?

DRUNK LADY: Miss, we need another round at this table.

BIG DUMB GUY: Miss, can you change the channel? We want to watch the game!

KIRSTY (NARRATOR): Oh, my God, a whole table of girls just got up and left without paying. I chase them into the parking lot:

KIRSTY: Hey! Hey! Excuse me, you forgot to pay your bill.

SMUG GIRL: Oh yeah, right. Here's a twenty—and another—we'll wait here for our change.

KIRSTY (NARRATOR): Change? You gotta be kidding me. You skip out on the bill, I am keeping your change.

DRUNK LADY: Miss, we need another pitcher!

BIG DUMB GUY: Miss, just get me the remote. We're missing the game!

HOT GIRL: Miss, I know you're busy and everything…but this is really lousy service.

KIRSTY (NARRATOR): It's 10PM on a Saturday night. We are getting slammed. By we I mean me. There is only me and the manager. The other waitress left early to go to a party. I'm running 100 tabs when I should have switched to cash and carry.

MANAGER WITH ACNE: Kirsty, these girls are complaining you stole their money.

KIRSTY: What? They tried to skip out on the bill! I am not giving back two bucks in change. It's my tip.

MANAGER: They want the two bucks, you gotta give it. And apologize.

KIRSTY: Screw this, just screw this! Here is my float, here is my key, here is my tray. You deal with this crowd. I quit…(in tears) And thanks for taking my side.

Scene 10: HOSTESS

KIRSTY (NARRATOR): On the bus, I open my mail. My mom has sent me a newspaper clipping. My former best friend Karen just got married. To a fellow accountant. After returning from their honeymoon in Hawaii, they will be opening a new office together. Pretty gown. I am the lunchtime hostess at Hy's Steak Loft. No more waitressing for me. You don't get tips as a hostess, but it's way better. You can wear nice clothes and nice shoes — no coffee, beer or grease will be spilling on my feet. The businessmen flirt, and the European waiters grumble but yield to my power. The hostess is in charge of assigning sections.

And this morning is special — I just taped an appearance on "Good Morning Sunrise," a local TV talk show. It's airing at 11:15, so…I slip into the bar to watch myself on the big-screen TV.

SFX: TV talk show interview.

KIRSTY (NARRATOR): Oh, God, I am talking way too fast and I am way too animated for television. I'm Betty Rubble on helium. But my hair is nice.

ITALIAN BARTENDER: Hey, is that you?

KIRSTY: No, it's my twin sister.

BARTENDER: Really? Your sister — she an actress or somethin'?

KIRSTY: Yes, no…the phone is ringing…I gotta go.

KIRSTY (NARRATOR): Why did I just lie? I should be proud of myself. I should have told all the staff to come watch me. Huh. I take a reservation for a party of three, and then I do the bank deposit. Every day, I walk the downtown streets with thousands of dollars of cash in a bag. Perhaps because I always come back, they offer me a full-time position in the office. I say no thanks. I've been on TV!

Scene 11: CARNY

Lies on a bunk bed, switches on a flashlight, directing the beam of light towards her face.

KIRSTY (NARRATOR): *(whispers)* I wake up to the sound of men's voices. It's the middle of the night, and I'm here all alone. I'm tucked into a makeshift bunk on a double-wide trailer. I'm a carny. I work, eat, and sleep on the midway. The carnies who work the thrill rides and games of chance are a tough bunch of ex-cons. Right now, there seems to be a small group of them talking about how to break into my rig.

Lights up as she flicks off the flashlight, stands up, and speaks in full voice as the Narrator.

KIRSTY (NARRATOR): This…is an old-timey photo booth — on wheels. The townies enter the dressing area, and we put them in costumes. In the daytime, it's Victorian families. On deck, we arrange furniture and pose them for a sepia-toned photograph from an antique camera. The babies look adorable in lace christening gowns and bonnets. Afternoons when business gets slow, Emme says, "Let's turn the tip." Carny lingo. That means we pretend to be customers — a few of us dress up and pose for pictures, the rest go outside to watch the show. Never fails to attract a crowd. Evenings are busy, as we set up Wild West couples over and over. The girlfriends always want to be Saloon Girls, with fishnet stockings, satin corsets and feather boas. And their drunken boyfriends all want to be cowboys with ten-gallon hats and six-shooter guns and rifles.

The lights dim. She resumes her place on the bed, flicking on the flashlight. She whispers.

KIRSTY (NARRATOR): And that's why these carnies are talking about breaking in. They want to steal our guns. If these guys weren't all high school drop-outs, they might have noticed that the guns are fake. Not that that matters at the moment. Someone says, "We need a ladder," and I can hear him light up a smoke.

SFX: a match strike and heartbeat.

KIRSTY (NARRATOR): I consider my options. I could get out of my bed, sneak under the canvas, and make a dash for the RV park, where Doug and Emmie are sleeping in their Winnebago. But the men might see me running and then I'd be caught in the open. Option two? Hide. My bed is like a coffin with a sideways lid. At night, I keep the lid propped open with a broken hockey stick. But during the day, it swings down and we display hats on the other side. If I can close it, nobody will know that I'm in here. It might get stuffy and hard to breathe, but that beats the alternative. Hold up the panel, dislodge the stick. A top hat falls and hits the carpet. The hinges are squeaking, the panel is heavy. It slips and closes with a bang. *(bangs the table—the heartbeat cuts out)* Shit! Shit!

Silence, breathing.

KIRSTY (NARRATOR): I lie very still. I don't move a muscle. I try not to breathe.

Pause.

KIRSTY (NARRATOR): I don't hear anything. Maybe they left. Maybe they heard the noise, thought there's a big burly security guy living on the rig, and took off. Let's hope.

Flashlight flicks off. Darkness.

Scene 12: LECTURER #2

The lecturer returns in lab coat and glasses.

LECTURER: How does a person find so many different kinds of day jobs? Relentless searching. Classified listings, bulletin boards, friends, colleagues, strangers. Craigslist, Monster — the internet made the searching faster and easier, but also endless. Looking for part-time work is a full-time job. Ironic. And being a self-employed actor — it's the same thing. You're always looking for "work" work. Looking for auditions, looking for an agent, looking for the next acting contract. A four-hour job, an eight-week job.

Starts to lose it, dropping her accent and revealing the anguished actress beneath.

KIRSTY (NARRATOR): Years and years of endless, non-stop, eyes-open, ears-to-the ground, relentless searching. It must be exhausting. How long can one keep this up — keep Believing in Acting? Forever? Is it even worth it?

Removes lab coat, pulls herself together.

Scene 13: TAXI CAB COUNTER - AIRPORT

SFX: buses, taxis, planes taking off.

KIRSTY (NARRATOR): A marketing firm needed people to go the airport and count cabs and limos for two long days. I don't know why. Some traffic survey. I am standing outdoors at Departures level, freezing to death, and sucking in exhaust fumes for ten hours straight. The taxis come and go, and the automatic doors slide open and closed. Must be doing a great job because they already offered me a full-time position. Indoors. As a manager. I'm always offered full-time and I always say no. This time I should really think about saying yes. I don't have a dental plan. Or a pension.

SFX: cell phone rings.

KIRSTY (NARRATOR): Oh! It's my agent! Hello… A role in a new musical?

SFX: fantasy music and twinkly lights start up.

KIRSTY: On Broadway? Opposite Hugh Jackman? You're kidding! *(music slowly dies)* She's kidding … Sure, I could babysit for you again.

Scene 14: FOCUS GROUP PARTICIPANT

KIRSTY (NARRATOR): In the elevator, I go over my story. I am an "arts administrator," I own a house, I have children, and I buy clumping cat litter. I don't own a cat and I don't have kids. This should feel like acting, but it just feels like lying. Sign in and wait. Always show up early—sometimes there are snacks. A little worried that I'll get busted. Actors are not allowed to do these and I just did a Fringe play that got really good reviews. We are escorted into a boardroom, a group of ten anxious-looking women of assorted age, size and ethnicity. That girl looks familiar—I saw her at an audition yesterday. She is a liar too! We avoid making eye contact. A blonde woman in a navy suit enters the room.

DIANE: Hello, ladies, my name is Diane and I work for Jump-Off Communications. Thank you so much for coming in! We are just going to have a friendly little chat. Now, see that big shiny mirror? There are some people on the other side of it. They are going to watch us and listen to what you have to say. No need to be nervous. Let's start by introducing ourselves.

KIRSTY (NARRATOR): Wonder if any of the marketing people behind the mirror go to the theatre. It's unlikely.

KIRSTY: Hi. I'm Chrissy. I'm an arts administrator and I sure love my kitty. Her name is Tabitha.

KIRSTY (NARRATOR): Diane hands out paper and a basket of crayons.

DIANE: Now, think about the last time you shopped for feminine hygiene products. What colour is the box that you most often buy? Pick a crayon, and draw it for me.

KIRSTY (NARRATOR): Feminine hygiene? I now regret introducing my pussy. I thought this focus group was for some new kind of kitty litter. Maybe I'm in the wrong room. Oh, well. I'm a girl, I can fake this. Is Playtex blue and Tampax pink, or is it the other way around? Ah, most of the other women are reaching for the pink crayons. I draw a pink box. I add flowers and hearts and a pony...

DIANE: Very good. Now turn your papers over...and put away your crayons.

Diane stands beside a flip chart, and uncaps a black marker.

DIANE: Now, ladies, I want you to think of words that describe the perfect panty liner. There's no wrong answer. ...Whatever you think.

VARIOUS WOMEN: Fresh? Clean? Dry.

DIANE: *(nods and writes down all the responses)* Good, good, yes, what else?

VARIOUS: Like a cloud. Like a marshmallow.

KIRSTY: Like a pillowy piece of heaven between your legs!

KIRSTY (NARRATOR): After ninety minutes, we are released. We line up politely and a receptionist hands each of us a plain white envelope. With a crisp, pink, fifty-dollar bill inside. Sweet. In the elevator, I write a list. Overdue phone bill — thirty-seven dollars. Groceries for the week — thirteen dollars. *(slowly)* Kraft Dinner, baloney, margarine, diet pop, eggs, one apple. *(scritch)* No eggs.

Scene 15: FOOD TASTER

KIRSTY (NARRATOR): Food tasting groups are an offshoot of focus groups. Not technically a job, and they don't happen very often — but it's the same deal — you have to qualify — you have to be employed — I mean, who wants to give food to someone who doesn't have a job? You and forty-nine other scruffy-looking people line up and take seats at paper-covered tables. The room is quiet with anticipation and embarrassment. Girls in hairnets parade from a kitchen with trays of paper plates, on each plate is a sample of a Subway sandwich.

You eat the sandwich slowly, inspecting it between bites, pretending that you care. And you fill out the questionnaire.

KIRSTY (NARRATOR): On a scale of one to ten, please rate the appearance of the bun. On a scale of one to ten, please rate the fluffiness of the bun. On a scale of one to ten, please rate the density of the bun. On a scale of one to ten, please rate the appearance of the dressing. On a scale of one to ten, please rate the viscosity of the dressing. On a scale of one to ten, do you believe that this pressed chicken product ever saw the inside of a henhouse?

KIRSTY (NARRATOR): And so on. Then the girls bring out another sandwich that looks and tastes exactly the same as the first one, but it's not, and you answer the same questions all over again. Two hours later, you're stuffed. You've got a twenty-dollar bill in a plain white envelope. And as long as you live, you never want to eat another Subway sandwich.

Scene 16: BACKGROUND

MALE 3RD A.D.: Quiet on set! Lock it down. Sound…rolling…background…action!

She walks across the stage, very simply.

A.D: Cut! Okay, going again. Reset.

She goes back to starting point.

A.D.: Okay, lock it down. Sound…rolling…background…action!

She makes the exact same cross again.

A.D.: Cut! Good. One more time. Reset.

As she goes back — we hear some mumbling from the A.D, then:

A.D: Lady with the purse. Yes, you. (*SFX: fantasy/circus music and twinkle lights start up*) Are you a trained actress? (*nods*) I thought so. Look, we just lost our leading lady. We are gonna need you to step into her part. The character is a supermodel. She has two love scenes, one with Brad Pitt, and one with George Clooney. The part pays ten million dollars. Do you think you could help us out?

KIRSTY: Yes! Sure! Of course!

She has ripped off her blouse.

A.D. (*loudly*) Lady with the Purse?

KIRSTY: Yes?

A.D.: I said, can you count five before you cross?

Happy music dies and twinkly lights fade.

KIRSTY: Sure.

Embarrassed, puts her blouse back on.

A.D.: Here we go. Quiet on set. Sound…rolling…background…action!

She counts to five, makes her third cross in a disappointed manner.

A.D.: And…that's a cut. Check the gate. We're gonna turn it around. Background, you can go to holding…We'll need you again in eight or nine hours.

Scene 17: MEET AND GREET STAFF

SFX: ship's blast.

KIRSTY (NARRATOR): Ah, the glamorous world of tourism. I am Meet and Greet Staff. It's going to be nine hours on my feet, and I got tendonitis from doing that Shakespeare play. My physiotherapist said my knees are pointing in the wrong direction. I told him I've been dancing all my life, what do you expect? I join a large group of women in navy suits, all trying to figure out how to tie our company neck scarves. We've been hired just for turnaround day. There will be four thousand tourists passing through the Cruise Ship Terminal. Most of them Americans. I am assigned to crowd control in entry hall B.

KIRSTY (NARRATOR): After an eerie silence, a long line of tourists begin to trudge towards me. They are loaded down like pack animals, dragging suitcases, bags of duty-free booze, and boxes of salmon. I am reminded of a zombie movie.

KIRSTY: Good morning. Please stay to the right. Good morning. Please stay to the right. Good morning. Please stay to the right.

KIRSTY (NARRATOR): Never point, always gesture with a closed hand. I direct them down a long hallway, where they will take an escalator to the main level. I decide to use my grade ten French just to frighten them a little.

KIRSTY: Bonjour! Allez à droite, s'il vous plait.

KIRSTY (NARRATOR): A security guard calls me aside.

EAST INDIAN SECURITY: Oh, golly, they are backed up downstairs like hamsters in a sock. Keep them here, and then let them through in small groups when I give you the signal.

KIRSTY: Sure.

She gestures to make the crowd stop.

ELDERLY NY TOURIST: What's wrong? Why can't we go? Is he a terrorist?

KIRSTY: We are just going to wait here for a minute, ma'am. For safety. It's a little crowded down there.

SAME TOURIST: Humph.

KIRSTY: Did you enjoy your cruise? Aren't the glaciers beautiful?

TOURIST: We have white tickets. We are express passengers.

KIRSTY: Yes, ma'am. Everyone here is an express passenger.

KIRSTY (NARRATOR): All of these Americans will get straight on a bus, which gets sealed, and drives across the border to Seattle. They don't have to go through customs if they don't set foot on Canadian soil.

TOURIST: They said no waiting. We paid extra for that. I have an artificial hip, you know, and my sinus is acting up.

KIRSTY: It will probably only be another minute. Say, where are y'all from?

TOURIST: First we waited two hours to get off the ship, and now we have to put up with this? We paid extra. I want a refund. Your cruise line is terrible!

KIRSTY: You are correct. My cruise line IS terrible. I will sell it immediately. After I fire all the staff. Now you may go ahead — to the front of the line. That's right ma'am, just you. Be careful on the escalator — wouldn't want to fall down and break your other hip. Bon voyage! Mange la merde!

Scene 18: DRAMA TEACHER

KIRSTY (NARRATOR): On the bus downtown, I open my mail. My mom sent me some newspaper clippings. My ex-best friend Karen? She looks great. And her children are very accomplished athletes. Pee Wee Goalie of the Year. All-Round Junior Gymnast. Good for them. Good for her.

LECTURER: *(quick transition — no costume change or special sound/lights)* Fun fact: any artistic-type person over the age of thirty who claims they don't have a day job is lying. You can be assured they pay the bills as an "acting coach" or "artistic director" or "theatre professor." Don't be fooled by the titles. These are day jobs.

KIRSTY (NARRATOR): I'm teaching drama — to a group of ten-year-olds. Ten-year-old *boys*. Did I say *teaching*? That's a bit of a stretch. I'm not a teacher. I'm more like a referee.

She blows a whistle.

KIRSTY: Okay, time out, Damien! In the corner — no — there's no arguing — testicles are very delicate organs — you should know that — Sirhan, do you need an ice pack? No? Okay, just lie down for a bit. IN THE OTHER CORNER. Brayden, we don't call each other names here — just because Sirhan is crying does not mean he is homosexual. And if he does grow up to be homosexual, he might be a talent agent or a casting director. Think about that. All right, everyone else — let's be zoo animals! And go… Jason, stop biting Chad… in our zoo, all the lions and the gazelles live together in perfect…oh, great, now there's blood. NEVER MIND! OKAY BOYS, PRETEND YOU ARE STATUES. FROZEN STATUES. STATUES DON'T MOVE AND THEY DON'T TALK. YES, I KNOW WE PLAYED THIS LAST WEEK. WE ARE GOING TO DO IT AGAIN!

KIRSTY (NARRATOR): I lock them in, and go to the ladies' washroom. For the next twenty-seven minutes, I study my lines for this national commercial I'm filming tomorrow — for a Subway sandwich campaign. Ha.

Scene 19: OFFICE TEMP

KIRSTY (NARRATOR): It's seven forty-five on a Monday morning and I am sitting behind a large desk, staring at the multi-line phone. It is my first day as a temp. I have never used a multi-line phone before. Raylene is giving me my orientation. Raylene says she started as a temp seven years ago, and has now worked up to executive assistant.

RAYLENE: Are you familiar with this phone system?

KIRSTY: (fudging) Uh, not this particular one. They're all a little bit different.

KIRSTY (NARRATOR): This, I find out later, is actually true.

RAYLENE: (with increasing speed) Okay. It's pretty easy. Just answer the call, press Transfer and the three-digit local, then hang up. You'll find all the locals here on these lists—employees are listed by first name alphabetically. Our technicians work in the lab downstairs, so you'll have to page them. To page, keep the call live, press Park, and then press Page, make your announcement, then press Release. Be sure to announce what line is holding. For example, "Renee, line 101, Renee line 101." Watch the light; if they don't pick up, go back to the caller and ask if they want to leave a message with you or on voice mail. If they want voice mail, press Send Message, the local, and Release. If a caller doesn't know who they want to speak to, just ask a few questions and try to narrow it down. Here is a list of our departments — inquiries about geological testing go to Roger, inorganic products go to Rameeza, petroleum research questions go to Ron — oh, but he's at the satellite office this week so you can forward his calls to Reiko, and any calls for Purchasing give to me. Also, if you need to use the washroom, you can forward the calls to me. Press Forward, 305, Forward. Don't forget to press Cancel when you're back. I'll pop around in a bit to give you the password for the postage meter and the online courier tracking program. Call me if you have a problem.

Raylene leaves.

KIRSTY (NARRATOR): I have a problem. I am way too old for a day job.

SFX: phone rings.

KIRSTY: Good morning, Coastal Inter-Tek Systems, please hold. *(ring, ring)* Good morning, Coastal Inter-Tek, please hold. *(ring, ring)* Coastal Inter-Tek, please hold. *(ring)* Please hold. *(ring)* HOLD! HOLD!

Panicked silence. Idea. She hits all the red flashing buttons repeatedly.

KIRSTY: Fuck off fuck off fuck off fuck off fuck off! Have a nice day. Fuck off.

She yanks the phone cord, wraps the phone and hides it in a box, exits hurriedly.

Scene 20: LECTURER #3

LECTURER: The average life span of a homo sapien is seventy-eight years. If they don't smoke. That's forty million minutes. The average person — if they are lucky enough to be employed — works forty hours per week for forty years — that's four million minutes. We live for forty million minutes, but we only work four million minutes. Work is only ten percent of your life. It just feels longer. Ah, but for the artist, creative work is one hundred percent of your life. Apparently, they are "born that way." Holding a day job does not indicate a lack of talent. It does, however, indicate the lack of value society places on artistic work. So, in conclusion...

Flips through the Acting Is Believing *book, looking for answers.*

LECTURER: Laughter is the best medicine. Leap and the net will appear. Ah. It's not the destination, it's the journey.

Scene 21: ACTRESS

KIRSTY (NARRATOR): Performing a lead role at a major regional theatre in my home town. Photo in the paper, talk show appearance, blah blah blah. Driving through the old neighbourhood in my mom's ancient Cadillac when I see the sign. Salisbury House. It's still there. The one I used to work at. My very first day job. I pull into the lot — parking this Caddy is like docking a cruise ship.

SFX: crowded restaurant.

KIRSTY (NARRATOR): The restaurant is exactly the same, but mostly it's the smell that takes me back. The aroma of grease trap and Mr. Clean hits me and I'm a teenager again. *(sits)* The lunch counter—who was that supervisor...she made me crawl underneath and scrape off lumps of chewing gum. She must have hated me. Cheese Nips, Egg Nips, it's all there.

KIRSTY: Wafer pie and a diet Coke, please.

KIRSTY (NARRATOR): Can see the cooks bent over the grill in their white paper hats. A lot of flirting happened over that pass-through. Me and Richard. Karen and Greg. We went to parties and drank and smoked with people much older than us. Pat was the old man at 24. The guys stole boxes of frozen steaks and hid them in the trunk of his red Mustang. We hung out in apartments furnished only with lawn chairs and foamies, were offered glasses of tap water. It was a whole new world to me. People who didn't live with their parents. People who didn't have…so many options. (eats wafer pie) Wonder if I could still carry five plates on one arm? A waitress says, "I'm cashed out, can you sign off on this, Richard?"

KIRSTY (NARRATOR): Richard? What a coincidence. Could it be? (sees him) Same voice. Brown hair, touch of gray. The acne is gone. But it's Rich, all right. My Rich… and he still works here? At Salisbury House? He catches my eye and comes over. He recognises me. The name tag on his chest says Richard, Manager. Brown eyes. He asks if I'd like some more Coke. Because refills are on the house! And he winks. He doesn't recognise me.

KIRSTY: Thank you. I'm fine.

KIRSTY (NARRATOR): He doesn't remember me.

She stands.

KIRSTY (NARRATOR): That's okay. It's not the destination. It's the journey.

Fade to black. Music.

About the playwright

Kirsten Van Ritzen is a professional actor who has received acclaim for performances across Canada. She has written sitcom, sketch, stand-up and several solo shows, and has two full-length dramas in the works. She is the author of a novel, *The Comedy Diaries*, and is Executive Producer of the TV series *The Broad Comedy Room*. Kirsten is a member of the Playwrights Guild of Canada and Writers Guild of Canada, as well as UBCP/ACTRA and CAEA. She lives in Victoria, BC. Visit her online at www.kirstenvanritzen.com

Interview

I had written or co-written six solo plays before I considered writing anything that was remotely autobiographical — the opposite of many actors, who excavate their own lives in their first solo plays. Probably because my middle-class upbringing was too boring to write about, or it was just way more fun to make stuff up. In late 2007, while spending a mind-numbing day as a proctor (a what?), it occurred to me that in my lengthy career as an actor, I had held many, many day jobs and perhaps it was time to put them all in a play: to offer up my humiliation and failure for public consumption. Kidding — she doth protest! I have enjoyed *plenty* of success as an actor. Many acting contracts even overlapped (rehearse by day, perform at night! Tra-la!).

But often there were short or long gaps to fill, and I could not in good conscience commit to full-time sweater folding, when I knew I had a fantastic summer gig — dancing! singing! emoting! — just around the corner. I became very good at sussing out short-term jobs where I wouldn't feel guilty about lying and quitting.

I began the outline by making a really, really long list of all those jobs, narrowing it down, then asking: how do I sum up any given experience in a brief scene? What was its essence? And what is the most entertaining way of telling each story? Since comedy comes from pain, and tragedy and disaster are *really* funny, I recalled the very worst moment of each job, then (in a few instances) unleashed myself from the truth of "what really happened" and wrote what I wished I might have said or done. Freeing myself from traditional narrative, I allowed each job/scene to find its own structure. My intention was to let the jobs tell the story, and not clutter it up with audition/acting anecdotes. "Kirsty's" backbone emerges as she matures and faces the folly of youthful ambition. (Goals: Win an Oscar before age thirty, marry Brad Pitt.) Not until rehearsals did my director point out that I had created nearly 30 different characters. Fun! After the first run, we cut several scenes (Proctor, Toilet Paper Rep, Retail Clerk/Bollywood Dance, Background #2); and I did a rewrite to bump up the funny: more fantasy, stronger scene-ending "buttons."

We expected actors and other artists to relate, and they did, but I was surprised at the enthusiastic reception from regular folks with "real jobs." I knew I hit a nerve when members of the audience lingered post-show, eager to tell me about their worst day job. Often it involved an abbatoir or tree-planting. Being an actress, of course, I had avoided work that involved dirt, blood or mosquitoes; I preferred playing "dress-up." (Whilst temping I'd pictured myself in an episode of *Ally McBeal*.) So I was happy to listen to horror stories from people who had just spent an hour laughing really hard at my own alleged suffering.

It also became clear that people who loved their real grown-up jobs and knew they were lucky to be employed still had moments where they felt incompetent, unappreciated, overwhelmed, bored to tears or ready to quit. They related to "Kirsty's" trials, and her actions provided a vicarious and satisfying reprisal — especially for former waiters. And temps. And anyone in customer service.

Postscript! A musician working Front of House told me she needed a monologue, and asked to use the first Lecturer speech. Curious, I asked what she was auditioning for. Turns out she had a job interview to sell hats. The manager of the hat store liked to hire creative people, and thus required potential staff to "audition." I was flattered, slightly appalled…and dubious. But now? If my play helps anyone land a minimum-wage day job in retail, I'd be pleased. If it reveals a few secrets of the hidden job market to the underemployed, I'd be thrilled. Or if an actress were to land an acting job with one of my monologues — I'd be ecstatic! But mostly I will be satisfied if my little "comedy about misery" makes people laugh.

Dear Penthouse

by Collin Doyle

Characters

TOM — an unsettled, unemployed security guard

Production History

Dear Penthouse premiered at the Edmonton International Fringe Festival in August of 2004.

Production Team:

TOM	Collin Doyle
FANTASY GIRL	Lora Brovold

DIRECTOR	Mieko Ouchi
STAGE MANAGER	Catherine Walsh
PRODUCTION DESIGN	Keving Corey
LIGHTING DESIGN	David Fraser
SOUND DESIGN	Dave Clarke

In black, the Beach Boys' "Put Your Head On My Shoulder" begins to play. After a moment...

Tom: In my dream, I come to the end of a path and there is a hot spring and steam is rising off the water. In the steam I can see shapes of people dancing, kissing, doing it, as it rises into the night and stars. And as I look up at the night, a star winks at me and says, look down at the water. Through the dancing fragments of steam, I see her.

Somewhere in this, lights reveal silhouettes moving to the music or narration.

Tom: She floats on her back in the water. I see her toes and knees peeking through the water. Some of her belly. Her breasts. Her face is covered in shadow. Her black hair stretches out from her like a living thing on the water. In my dream, she reaches out her hand, beckoning me to come in. I step into the water and I feel heat burning through my feet, my legs, my crotch. She moves towards me, her hair covering her face, her lips shining. I see the dark pink of a nipple and then her hair sways to cover it.

I want this to be perfect.

Lizard: *(whispering)* "Hey, buddy."

Tom: At the edge of the water my lizard sits warming himself on a rock. He smiles at me. He nods as if to say —

Lizard: *(whispering)* "This is your chance."

Tom: In my dream, she is in front of me. I want to say so much to her. Her hair moves across her face and she smiles with perfect teeth and lets out a perfect sigh. And it is so hot, like my feet are about to explode hot, and I have nothing to say.

Lizard: *(whispering)* "Hey, buddy, think of the possibilities."

Tom: At the edge of the water my lizard rolls on his back, does his trick, and opens his mouth and makes his head disappear.

Lizard: *(whispering)* "It's only...a dream."

Tom: I look at my dream girl.

There are so many possibilities.

And my feet are tingling.

And all I have to do is choose.

And my feet are burning.

And she reaches out to touch me.

And my feet explode.

The sound of the Metro train blasting into the station. Lights up on Tom pacing. He is slightly frustrated.

TOM: So. This is what happened. I had been waiting in the store for the manager to put the new issue of *Penthouse* on the stand. It was 6:00 in the evening and usually the new issue arrives around 5:30 and is on the rack fifteen minutes later. When I got to the store it was exactly 5:45 and the magazine was still in the box. Busy day, I assumed, even though there were no other customers in the store and the manager was idly stocking another shelf. So I decided to wait for him to put the new issue out.

I don't like to disturb people just to get what I want. I roamed around the store for a while and checked out the current issues of *Hustler*, *Swank*, *Playboy*, *Jugs*, *Big Mamas*, *Chickenhawk*, *Barely Teens*, *Cougars*, *Vixens*, *Moist*, *Fat* and *Filthy*. They didn't interest me much. Really.

Okay. See, I'm a *Penthouse* man. *Penthouse* isn't as dirty as *Hustler*, but it's not as snobby as *Playboy*. It's the magazine for men who don't like airbrushed models and don't like in-depth photographic studies of a girl's you-know-what. It's for the man who likes a little sleaze with some class. Okay. I don't buy it for the articles. Though they have some good ones.

The new issue of *Penthouse* is released the first Tuesday of every month. And every month I come to this store at this Metro station at the exact same time to pick up my copy. It's the only time I visit this store.

It didn't look like the manager was going to finish stocking that shelf any time soon. So I asked him if he could just grab me a copy. He squinted at me and told me to come back in half an hour.

"Couldn't you just take one out of the box?"

MANAGER: No, I have to count them first. Make sure I got all my copies.

TOM: "This is a convenience store. It's supposed to be convenient."

Okay. Now my thinking was he could just give me my copy and mark it off for when he counts them later. I was about to say this when I picked up his Vibes: He was fifty-two. He had owned this store for the last thirty years. Twelve-hour days of the same dusty shelves. 20-ounce bottle of rye at night. The beeping of a till in his dreams. Two, maybe three years, tops, it all ending with a mountain of empty packages of Skittles and a shotgun to the head. Bad Vibes. I couldn't stay in the store. So I said "forget it"…and told him, "I will be back in thirty minutes to get my copy!"

I left the store and stood just in front of it. I watched people rush by me on their way to the turnstile and ticket booth and the train, or rushing in the other direction towards the exit. Their Cold Blue Vibes squeezing past each other: I hate my family. I despise my boss. I can't make it one more day. I am so lonely.

It's a cruel world… After a while, I was bored.

I had noticed the photo booth a long time ago, and I had always wanted to get some pictures of myself. I hadn't had a picture taken in five years or more and I was curious how I would look. Okay. See, a picture is different than looking into a mirror. A picture is an image you can never change. If you got one eye closed or snot hanging out of your nose, you're stuck with that look. A picture is a gamble. But in a mirror you can kind of move your face until you look better or more pleasing or heroic or handsome. For me, I just lower my head a little and turn it to the right. That's how I look good.

So, being bored, I crossed the concourse to get a couple of snapshots. I sat down in the booth. Closed the green curtain. Popped three loonies in.

> *Tom smiles at the camera. Nothing. He changes his pose. Nothing. He looks at the instructions on the side. Immediately the bulb flashes four times, blinding Tom.*

TOM: Son of a bitch!

> *Beat.*

TOM: I now had three minutes to wait for the photos and I wasn't sure if I should just keep sitting in the booth or if I should wait outside. I didn't want people to notice me sitting in the booth with no pictures being taken, but on the other hand, I didn't want people to notice me leaning against the booth waiting for pictures of just myself.

See, photo booths are like a group thing. I've always noticed groups of people trying to cram themselves into one of these booths, laughing and having a good time. I've also noticed people who are by themselves and get them done. These people always give off Sad Vibes. I don't want anybody to feel sorry for me. I decided to wait outside of the booth.

When I got out of it, I saw the manager, directly across the concourse, putting out the new *Penthouse*. He had lied to me. He was putting it out earlier than he said and now I had another two minutes to wait for my pictures before I could buy my *Penthouse*…

Okay. Something I didn't explain earlier is I like to buy the first copy put on the stand at this particular store. It's a good luck charm for the month. Whenever I buy it, I always have a good month. But when I don't get that copy, it's usually a shitty month, and the last five months had been kind of good. Better than average. And now, while I was waiting for the pictures, somebody could come along and buy my copy and fuck my whole month. I was stuck. Well, I wasn't really stuck. All I had to do was rush over and buy my copy and then rush back to get my pictures. If I did it fast enough, I might even be back before they came out of the chute on the side. It was like a race, and I liked to have races with myself.

So, I ran as fast as I could across the concourse to the store. I grabbed my *Penthouse* triumphantly. Winner! The manager looked at me with his Bad Vibe eyes. He took his time going around to the till and punching in the price of the magazine.

MANAGER: $7.95.

TOM: He said to me as if I had fucked and killed his mother. Anyways, having my *Penthouse*, I raced out of the store. Son of a bitch! The pictures were in the slot. If it hadn't been for the manager, I would have won.

So, having lost the race, I strolled across the concourse to the booth as I thumbed through my *Penthouse*. A couple of lesbian pictorials. Those were always interesting. Some shaving cream action. Some girl-with-guy pictures. Shaving cream? Yeah.

When I looked up, there was a woman in front of the photo booth and she was picking up my pictures. I watched as she first looked at the pictures and then put them in her purse. She was stealing my pictures… I was about to yell, "Stop… thief!" or, "Hey…you!" when she began to walk away. I didn't say anything.

Okay. See, I was curious why she took my photos. Did I look handsome in the pictures? Intriguing? Was there a glint in my eye? What caused her to take them, to take me, and put me in her purse? And besides that, why would she steal photo booth pictures? It's pointless to take the pictures of somebody you don't know. It's like taking someone's contact lenses or false teeth. And she was disappearing.

So I followed her, this plain and uninteresting-looking woman, someone I would have never noticed in a crowd. She was like a phantom woman that seemed to disappear as she moved through the people. I couldn't get her Vibes.

I followed her through the turnstile and down to the platform to wait for the Metro. She leaned against a wall…and disappeared. The Metro came. I searched for her brown jacket, her brown hair, her chubby body. The doors of the train opened, people began to push on and off of the train. I searched and searched. Where was she? …Her blue eyes. I latched onto her eyes as they floated towards the train. I knew she couldn't disappear again; I had her blue eyes.

She went through the last door of the car. I went through the middle one. I sat with my back towards her. I could see her reflection in the window. She pulled a book from her purse and began to read. It was some book about a serial killer. Since it looked like we had some time until we hit her stop, I decided to read my *Penthouse*.

Okay. I like to read the letters about people's sexual experiences first. Yeah, I know they're made up. I even tried to write one of my own this one time: it was about a guy…who's having sex…with a girl…

Okay. After I read the letters, I then read the reviews of the recently released porno videos. I don't have a VCR, but the reviews can be pretty funny. Okay. After this I look at the photo layouts. But I didn't get a chance to look at the photos; I didn't even get to the reviews. I was only on the third letter when I noticed she was getting ready to get off the train.

The Metro came to a stop, and I continued to follow this stranger. She had my pictures and I had her blue eyes. That was our connection. When she took my pictures, we connected. I had to follow.

So, up the stairs, through the turnstile, more stairs, and then onto the street. Down the street, a left, a right, another right, one more right and we were at her place. The whole time I followed from an extreme distance. But I think if I had walked right next to her, she wouldn't have noticed me. She was in her own world, maybe thinking about me in my pictures. Maybe. Yeah.

She stopped…went up the stairs…and through the door…of a three-story building. All the windows in the building were dark. I waited by a tree. All twelve windows were dark. Which light would come on? I would just wait to find out and leave. Which light would come on? Top floor, main floor, or basement? She had probably just now put her bag down. Not the main floor. It had to be top or bottom. She had probably just taken off her jacket and shoes. Top? Basement? I bet it's the basement. No! I bet it's the top. Come on, top. Come on, top. Come on, top…Go, top, Go, top. Go, top… Go, to —

A light comes on. A basement light.

Tom: Son of a bitch! There was a tiny iron fence separating a small patch of grass from the sidewalk. Bushes blocked two windows. The street was empty. I went to step over the tiny iron fence.What was I doing? Following this woman home was one thing, but now I was breaking a law. I'm very big on privacy. I always keep my curtains closed in my room. To violate someone's privacy is sickening. And I was going to do that. I was going to look into her private world.

Her curtains were open. I stepped over the fence. Okay. If her curtains had been closed, I wouldn't have looked in. Okay, if they had been halfway closed, I wouldn't have looked in.But they were all the way open. Wide open. She wasn't worried about her privacy. Basement suite and she leaves her curtains open? She obviously didn't care. So it wasn't really a violation, and I needed to know what she was going to do with my pictures.

I crawled between the bushes and then I peered through her window. I was looking into her living room and kitchen. The other window probably looked into her bedroom. I would not violate that space. Honest. Branches from the bushes were blocking me, but not enough to hide me if she were to look directly out the window. If anybody were to walk by right now they would have seen my legs sticking out of the bushes. I was risking a lot, but she had my pictures in her purse. Me. A piece of me was in that room.

She no longer hid as she sat in her home. I watched her in her living room; surrounded by an old TV, brown appliances, a couch, a chair, and some pictures on the walls. I watched her sit on the couch, my pictures nowhere in sight, relaxing after a long day. She took off her socks and smelled them and then made a face and then laughed at herself for smelling her socks. I watched her make supper: spaghetti with meat sauce. She judged if her spaghetti was cooked by throwing it at the wall. She did this eight times. Changing her throw each time she did it. One time she pretended she was a major league pitcher in a high stakes game, throwing the spaghetti like it was a hundred-mile-per-hour fastball. The crowd going wild when she struck out the batter and her taking in their cheers: "Yaaaa!"

I watched her watch TV as she ate her spaghetti and drank a glass of wine. She watched *Jeopardy*, and each time she got a question right she would take a sip of her wine. I watched her wash dishes. She brushed her hair away from her face and got dish soap on her temple. I watched her eat ice cream. Häagen-Dazs ice cream. Five spoonfuls of ice cream is all it took for me to love her.

I touched the window. "Let me in." Let me into your life. Let me into your world. She looked up. Had she heard me? She was looking around the living room. I had to get away. I forced myself out of the bushes. I stepped back over the fence, back to the sidewalk, to the cold concrete.

"I love you." I could see her looking up from her book again, hearing my words over the iron fence, the grass, the bushes, and through the window. I love you. I turned and floated back down the street. Heading towards the Metro, but my mind was still in her apartment, lying next to her on the couch.

I floated onto the Metro thinking of what she smelled like. I floated off at my stop, passed the store where the manager was sending out his evil gremlins. I fought those off and sent thoughts of love at him. I thought those would piss him off. I floated up the stairs and out into the night air.

IT WAS CHILLY!

What was her name? Beth. She looked like a Beth. I floated to the door to my home. I floated past my roommate Charlene. I said, "HELLOOO!" She has never spoken a word of English to me. Ever. I floated past my other roommate Helen's door; I could hear her whispering her prayers. I floated downstairs to my room.

> *"In my Room" by the Beach Boys begins to play. Tom does a striptease to the song.*

TOM: I put the new issue on top of the stack of old issues. It would be a good month. Okay. I have five years' worth of *Penthouse* magazine. Five years of letters and luck. I had bought the first issue on the spur of the moment. I had never looked at a nudie magazine before this, but there was something about the woman on the cover that turned me on. It seemed like she had been caught alone while contemplating something, maybe she had heard the click of the camera or the brush of the curtain being moved out of the way, and she had turned just a little to pose. She knew somebody was watching her and it was okay…so I bought it.

These are one of my treasures. I don't have many. I have some Secret Admirer notes hidden in a drawer…I was too afraid to send them. I have a picture of my grandma and me; it's tucked between my mattress and box spring. I have a wooden nickel a next-door neighbour gave me for shovelling his walk. There are not many wooden nickels in the world. I keep it in my left pocket on Mondays, Wednesdays, and Fridays. I keep it in my right pocket the rest of the week. And finally, I have my lizard skull.

Okay. A long, long time ago, when I was little, I was far away from here in another place, a backyard actually. It was the only place to escape to, my jungle, because the grass was never mowed and the weeds would grow until they were chest-high. I would look for dinosaurs: a brontosaurus, or a stegosaurus, or a monstersaurus. Then one day, I found, deep down in the dirt, a tiny skull of…a lizard. I knew it wasn't a dinosaur, but it would do. How long had this skull been hiding in the dirt, waiting for me to find it? And if I held the skull at a certain angle in the light, it looked like my lizard was agreeing with me. And if I held the skull at a different angle, it looked like my lizard was disagreeing. I would ask him questions. Yes. A twist of my wrist. No. "Will we be moving soon?

LIZARD: *(whispering)* "Yes".

TOM: "Will he come home tonight?"

LIZARD: *(whispering)* "No."

TOM: "Should I pretend I'm sleeping?"

LIZARD: *(whispering)* "Yes."

TOM: Later, in school, somebody told me, after I showed it to him and he had punched me, that my lizard skull was actually a squirrel skull. It didn't matter. I had made it a lizard. These are my possessions: some letters, a photo, a wooden nickel, my *Penthouse* magazines, and a lizard skull.

Charlene saw my collection once. She got all flustered and embarrassed when she saw the top issue of the stack. I thought she might say something to me. One word of English, but she just backed quickly out of the room.

I wouldn't think of showing them to Helen. She has already told me I'm going to hell. She asked me why I didn't go to church and I told her I didn't believe in God. She told me that I was going to hell in a handcart. "Hand-basket," I said, "It's hell in a hand-basket." She slammed the door in my face. She'll never see my collection. Maybe Beth will.

Oh, God, Beth. Beautiful Shy Beth! Tomorrow, I would get up early and follow her and find a moment to talk to her. I would tell her how she had my pictures, and it was all right, and I knew she didn't steal them; it was a connection.

> *Lights to black. "Wouldn't It Be Nice" or "God Only Knows" by the Beach Boys plays. A single light comes up on Tom.*

In my dream, Beth is sitting on a sleeping bag. It's July 1st and all around her people are lying on blankets and looking up at the night; waiting for the explosions. There is the ringing bell of an ice-cream cart, the smell of sun-baked skin. There is laughter because everyone knows it's a holiday.

Beth grabs my hand and squeezes it as I sit down next to her. My lizard looks down at us from a tree. He winks at me.

In my dream, I know the fireworks are going to start. There is a buzz and everyone holds their breath. Waiting. And I turn to Beth and I'm going to say to her, "Are you ready?" But as Beth turns to me, she smiles and she has no eyes. She has blank spaces where her blue eyes should be. In my dream, everything would be perfect if Beth had eyes. I could kiss her if she had eyes.

> *Fireworks and explosions.*

Beth?

> *Lights up full.*

TOM: I'm lying in my bed. I can hear the tick of my clock, the hum of the furnace, the pops of the floor expanding and contracting, cars driving by on the street. My room seems really small. My bed seems really small. I'm really small. Nothing Beth would ever want. Why would she want to be with an unemployed security guard? I can remember her hair, her nose, even the tiny scar she has by her right eye. I can't remember her eyes.

LIZARD: *(whispering)* "Why so glum, chum?"

TOM: My lizard is sitting on top of my TV. He licks his lips.

          "Is this a dream?"

LIZARD: *(whispering)* "Maybe. Does it matter?"

TOM: "No."

LIZARD: *(whispering)* "Sooo?"

TOM: "I can't remember Beth's eyes."

My lizard paces back and forth on the TV set.

LIZARD: *(whispering)* "What did her eyes look like?"

TOM: "I don't —"

LIZARD: *(whispering)* No, no, just think of their shape.

TOM: I try to imagine the shape of her eyes. I can kind of see them.

           My lizard sticks out his tongue and shapes them into Beth's eyes. They are blue.

           The sound of an alarm clock.

           Beth.

           Tom gets dressed. He checks his watch to see how long it took to get dressed.

TOM: In eighteen minutes I shit, showered, shaved and I was out the door to the Metro. At the Metro station everyone's Vibes seemed to be turned up by my love for Beth. I watched them bounce off the walls and echo back. Happy Vibes. Cuddly-Wuddly Vibes. Lovey-Dovey Vibes.

           A Metro ride sitting next to a little boy. He gave off Vibes that said, "I've got cookies." The Metro came to Beth's stop and I strolled off. I strolled up the stairs and through the turnstile, more stairs, and then on to the street.

           IT WAS HOT!

           A man with a bushy moustache smiled at me; he knew I was in love. I strolled down the street, the sun was out and smiling, a left, hardly any clouds in the sky, a right, the birds were singing, another right, there was the smell of fresh baked bread in the air, one more right, and I was at her place.

           I arrived at the building as she came out the front door. Everything went quiet: cars and people stopped; Vibes froze in the air. I could smell her perfume and I could hear her heartbeat. This was the moment. Picnics and fireworks. All the possibilities in the world. I would tell her now.

           "Beth, I— I— I— I... Beth?" She continued walking down the street towards the Metro.

           "Beth?"

           She hadn't heard me call her name. Unless, of course, Beth really wasn't her name. It was the name I gave her!

           I followed her back down the street, back to the Metro, back onto the train; thinking of a way to get her to look at me. She had her face in her book again and was hiding from this world. Keeping her eyes in the book or on the ground or out the window. And I didn't want to tell her I loved her here, on this stinking train.

           The doors opened at the stop where we first met. She got out and I followed: past the manager in his small store, onto the escalator, and up onto the street. I was right behind her. We were heading in the direction of my place. Were we going to my place? We passed a beggar and she stopped. She put a dollar in his hand, not in the hat he was holding out, but his hand. His Vibes changed for a second from helpless to happy. That's what I wanted. That change. I put a dollar in the homeless man's hand, touching his palm where Beth's hand had touched…

I'm in a picture booth. The curtain is closed and it's very warm. I can see my reflection in the lens of the camera. A hand comes through the curtain. It's Beth. She runs her hand through my hair and onto the back of my neck. My hands are shaking. I pull her into the booth. She sits in my lap. I wrap my arms around her. I put my hand inside her coat and she is wearing…nothing. She puts three dollars into the machine.

> *The bulb flashes.*

She kisses me, puts her tongue in my mouth. "I want you," I say to her.

> *The bulb flashes.*

She sways her hips over me. I bite her nipple. I'll be whatever you want.

> *The bulb flashes.*

I'll be whatever you want.

> *The bulb flashes.*

I'll be whatever you want.

HOMELESS MAN: *(drunk)* You'll have to give me more than a buck to do that.

TOM: What? Beth? She was disappearing into the mall. I followed her. I followed her down the escalator and into the food court as old people leered. Old people smoking cigars, pipes, and cigarettes as they pushed their oxygen tanks from one food court table to another. I followed her out of the food court, heading towards the grocery store. An old lady stepped in front of me, smiled at me.

OLD LADY: Excuuuse meee.

TOM: I pretended not to hear her.

OLD LADY: Excuuuuuse meeeeee!

TOM: Beth was getting further away from me. I couldn't lose her right now. "What? What do you want?"

OLD LADY: Do…you…know…the…*(an epic pause)*…tiiiime?

TOM: The time? The love of my life was disappearing into the grocery store, and she wants to know the time. "No, I don't know the time. So why don't you go die!"

Tom gasps and covers his mouth.

I didn't mean to say the last part.

"Sorry."

Tom races into the grocery store. Sounds of a grocery store.

TOM: She was gone. She wasn't in the vegetables, or the dog food/laundry, or the coffee/crackers. I made my way, checking aisle after aisle. Searching for Beth. Up and down. I was in the bakery when I finally found her. She was wearing a white uniform and carrying a cash tray. A cashier. She looked fabulous in her uniform.

I don't know why *Penthouse* has never devoted an issue to the cashiers of grocery stores. She headed up to the front of the store. She carried her purse under one arm. She went to a lane. She put her purse under the counter and the cash tray into the till. She turned her light on. Number eight flashed. My favourite number!

Okay. I would purchase some food…for our meal. I would take the food to her lane and slowly unload it on to the conveyor belt. Watch it travel to her. She would look up as she swipes an item across the scanner. Our eyes would connect. She would let out a sigh and try to speak. I would whisper, "I love you." She would smile with her eyes.

BETH: Sexy. I love you too.

TOM: I grabbed a shopping cart and began to shop for our…feast. Okay. She liked spaghetti; she must like Italian food. I grabbed a frozen lasagna. I grabbed some garlic bread. I grabbed a bottle of wine. It was a white wine from Chile. I grabbed a corkscrew. I grabbed… How many candles does it take to light up a room? I grabbed eight candles and eight candleholders. And finally…a box of condoms. Trojans. A twenty-four pack. And then it was off to lane number eight for a meeting with destiny.

There was an old lady getting her groceries scanned at Beth's aisle. She only had a few items. It was the woman I told to die. I hid behind a flower display until the woman was gone. I grabbed some flowers. I walked up to the conveyor belt. Beth hadn't looked at me yet. She was busy changing the till tape. It was good she hadn't. I wanted it to be just the right moment. I put the flowers down on the conveyor belt. I put the eight candles and eight candleholders down. I put the bottle of wine down. She finished changing the tape. I put the corkscrew down. I put the garlic bread down. The flowers moved towards her. I put the frozen lasagna down. Her hand moved towards the flowers. I put the condoms down. She swiped the flowers across the scanner. The candles moved towards her. She smelled the flowers. Perfect. She would look up now. She put the flowers gently into a bag. She didn't look up.

She didn't look up as she swiped the candles, the candleholders, the wine, the corkscrew, the bread, the lasagna, or the condoms! I would have to bring her out of this. I grabbed a caramel chocolate bar. I walked up beside her, only the counter separated us. I wanted so much for her to look at me. She stacked the plastic bags next to each other. Still not looking at me.

BETH: $42.37.

TOM: Beth had a beautiful voice. I saw her nametag: Josie. "Josie." I held the caramel chocolate bar in front of her turned-down head. "I have one more item." She went to take the chocolate bar from my hand. Our hands touched. I felt her Vibes shoot up my arm. Kissing. Warm sand. A small house. Two kids. Growing old. We began to speak at the same time. I stopped myself. I would let her say it to me first.

JOSIE: (*friendly*) You have to let go of the chocolate bar if you want me to swipe it.

TOM: "I love you too — What?"

JOSIE: I can't swipe it if you're holding it.

TOM: "Don't you know who I am?"

She looked at me, finally taking me in.

JOSIE: No, I don't.

TOM: "It's me." Her smile started to fade. Two old people began loading their groceries onto the conveyor belt. Brittle bone death Vibes traveled towards me. Something shifted. "It's Me! ME!"

JOSIE: Shaking her head. Flustered. "I'm sorry, I don't know you."

TOM: "The pictures."

JOSIE: "Sir, calm down. I don't know what pictures you mean."

TOM: "The goddamn pictures from the machine."

My feet started to tingle. A manager began to walk towards us from the other side of the store.

"You stole my fucking pictures, Beth — From the Metro — I was going to make you lasagna — "

I felt the manager's warm hand on my shoulder. "Get away from me."

The old people backed away from now unlucky number eight. Beth was shaking. I was shaking.

"Why did you take them?"

I knew the customers in the store were looking at me, watching me, staring at me.

"Why did you take them?" I said to Josie. Her Vibes screamed "please leave me alone."

She didn't know who I was.

"Get out right now," the manager said.

I walked out of the store. I would have run, but more people would have noticed me. I wandered into the food court. All of the old people glared at me. The smoke from their cigarettes, cigars, and pipes hovered above their heads and formed their thoughts: Loser. Fool. Hopeless. Stalker. Reject.

I wandered onto the escalator. It immediately stopped as I got on it. It figured. I walked up the metal stairs, each step squeaked out an insult: Fuck-face. Shithead. Dink. Cocksucker. Asshole.

I wandered to the exit. A homeless man held the door open with one hand and held his other hand out to me. I didn't give him anything.

I wandered out into the lonely city. It was raining. It figured. I didn't care if I got wet. I didn't care at all. I wandered down the street as fat teardrops of rain landed on me. Soaking me. In each teardrop I could see a different possibility: Beth waiting for her picture to be taken.

Splash.

Beth smiling.

Splash.

Beth closing her eyes.

Splash.

Beth floating in the water, laughing.

Splash.

Beth's blue eyes.

Splash.

Beth rejecting me.

Splash.

Beth embarrassed.

Splash.

Beth crying.

Splash.

Beth…

TOM: All the teardrops, raindrops, formed a giant puddle in front of the steps to my rooming house. I could see my reflection in the puddle. Not handsome. Not ugly. Just me, soaking wet.

I wandered past Charlene in the kitchen.I wandered past Helen, praying in her room. I wandered downstairs to my room and past my five-year collection of *Penthouse* magazines. It hadn't been lucky.

LIZARD: *(whispering)* "Hey, chum, why so glum?"

TOM: My lizard sits on the window ledge. The curtains closed behind him.

"I got the Vibes wrong."

My lizard's ancient green eyes stare at me.

LIZARD: *(whispering)* "It's all how you choose to look at things."

TOM: My lizard yawns; his eyes change briefly from green to red and then back.

LIZARD: *(whispering)* "You want to see a trick?"

TOM: "Sure."

A tiny flame puffs from his mouth and my curtains catch on fire and I watch them burn away and reveal the world outside.

Beth is standing there, pressing my photo booth pictures against the window. She is soaking wet. Her hair is plastered to her face, her lips shining.

I feel heat burning through my feet.

Beth smiles.

She gives off Good Vibes.

There are so many possibilities.

"Good Vibrations" by the Beach Boys begins to play.

My lizard winks at me.

My feet are about to explode.

I choose.

Lights fade to black.

About the playwright

Collin Doyle is an Edmonton-based writer. His play *The Mighty Carlins* premiered at Workshop West in January of 2008. Nakai Theatre in Whitehorse produced a second production in the spring of 2009. Persephone Theatre in Saskatoon produced a third production in February of 2012. *The Mighy Carlins* was the winner of the Discovery Category of the Alberta Playwriting Competition in 2004, and received the Sterling Award for Outstanding New Play in 2008. His play for teens, *Routes,* premiered in the fall of 2009. Concrete Theatre toured *Routes* to high school audiences in Alberta, Saskatchewan, and Ontario. *Routes* received a Sterling Award for Outstanding Production for Young Audiences; it also received a Dora Award for Outstanding Production for Young Audiences. His play *Slumberland Motel* won the main category of the Alberta Playwriting Competition in 2006. His plays *Dear Penthouse* and *Nighthawk Rules* (with James Hamilton) were critical and popular successes at the Edmonton Fringe in 2004 and 2005. *Nighthawk Rules* received two Sterling Awards for Outstanding Fringe Production and Outstanding New Fringe Work. His new play, *Let the Light of Day Through,* won the Alberta Playwriting Competition in 2012. Theatre Network in Edmonton will produce *Let the Light of Day Through* in the spring of 2013. Collin is a graduate of the National Theatre School of Canada.

Interview

It's the fall of 1996. I'm twenty-one. I'm in Montreal. I'm in my first year of acting at the National Theatre School of Canada. I'm living in the McGill ghetto, renting a second-floor room in, basically, a boarding house. There are two other tenants living on the second floor with me. One is a woman from China. She works as a researcher. The second is a woman from Australia. She's here on a student exchange program. Besides my new theatre school classmates, I know absolutely no one else. I am alone. I do not speak a word of French. I remember being in high school in Edmonton and someone suggested that I should take a French class as one of my options. I said to that person: Why would I ever need French?

Anyway.

I'm in one of those first-year acting classes where you're doing theatre exercises that are somehow vaguely related to acting. I guess if you do enough these exercises in the first semester everything will make a lot more sense in the second semester when you pick up an actual play. For today's exercise, all us first-year students had to bring in a photograph of ourselves. One of my classmates, Amy Sloan, races into the class, late. She apologizes, blaming her lateness on the photo booth at the Place Des Arts metro station. I guess she'd gone through all the steps at the photo booth—put in the money, smiled for the camera, four flashes, and then she waited for the photos to develop. After a few minutes, the photos still hadn't developed. I guess there was a phone number on the side of the booth to call when you had a problem with your photos. Frustrated, Amy went to the payphone to call the photo booth company and complain. She got an answering machine. She left a message where she said something about not getting her "fucking pictures." She headed back to the photo booth. She found her photos waiting in the chute on the side. She tells this story in our acting class. I think: What if someone had stolen the pictures while she went to make the phone call? I think: Why would anyone steal a stranger's pictures from a photo booth?

Anyway.

It's August of 2004. I'm twenty-nine. I'm performing in *Dear Penthouse* at the Edmonton Fringe Festival. It's going well: long line-ups for tickets, sold-out houses, and great reviews. It's been eight years from the first draft to this staged production. I've learned a lot since I originally wrote this strange little hybrid of short story and play—inspired by my classmate's story and my lonely first year in Montreal. Since then, I've rewritten the play, added the fantasy dream girl sequences, changed the ending over and over, and added the talking lizard. The lizard was taken from a writing exercise I had done at theatre school and grafted on to *Dear Penthouse*. In rehearsing the play, I learned how to cut and rewrite on the fly; we had a rule that if a line in the play was actable then the line would be cut. I learned that if you call a play *Dear Penthouse*, some audience members might assume it's a dirty little play about some guy's sexual experiences. In fact, before the reviews came out, some people did attend in the hopes of seeing a dirty little play. They were disappointed when the only nudity on stage was a chubby white guy in his underwear. I learned to not explain the play too much, let there be questions.

People often ask me, "Why does the girl take the pictures?" I know why she takes the pictures, but after talks with my director, Mieko Ouchi, I decided to keep it a mystery, let the audience imagine, let them have their own fantasies…Why do you think she takes the pictures?

Sunnyside Café

by Pam Calabrese MacLean

Characters

EVA — a woman in her fifties

Setting

The Sunnyside Café, a small diner.

Note: Mama's voice (done by Eva) is raspy and heavily accented (Eastern Europe)

Production History

Sunnyside Café was produced by Forerunner for the Atlantic Fringe Festival NS (2009); Ship's Company Main Stage NS (2011); Happy Valley-Goose Bay, Labrador Lawrence O'Brien Center (2011). Eva was played by Sherry Smith and Lee J. Campbell directed. Jenny Munday (PARC) was dramaturge.

The playwright would like to thank PARC (Sunnyside Café was developed at the Playwrights Atlantic Resource Centre's 2009 Playwrights' Colony, in Sackville, NB), and Ottawa Little Theatre, without whom there would be no production history.

There is a table with three chairs around it. The table has a red gingham tablecloth. Eva, wearing a waitress uniform, enters stage right, crosses the stage, and exits stage left. Eva enters stage left, carrying a tray of salt shakers and an old teapot full of salt. Eva takes her shoes off and sits before she begins to fill the shakers. Her toes poke through a hole in her pantyhose.

EVA: This is the last thing I do Saturday night. Fill the salt and peppers. My kind of task, simple. Black & white. No real choices. Well, no real consequences.

Safe. Like walking.

No matter where you go, how far, how often, how fast. If you're walking, you always have one foot on the ground.

I like having one foot on the ground.

Surprises me that I loved to dance. But I did. When I was a young woman and if tips were good I'd play the jukebox while I worked and sometimes I'd be done all my jobs and there'd be music left over and I'd dance.

There was never anyone here but me. No one to lift or twirl me. So, really, just fancy walking.

I've lived nearly my whole life eighty-nine steps from the Sunnyside Café's front door.

Mama and I came here when I was two weeks old.

Some of it I truly remember and some I know is just Mama.

She told how in the beginning, she'd bound me tight, left me to go out and wash other people's dishes, racing home from the Sunnyside Café, across Melbourne Street, up the dark stairs to feed and change me. How later she kept me in a wooden crate that her boss, Mr. Frank, she called him, let stand beside the double steel sink.

One of my first memories. The hissing water, the clatter of the dishes and the black lines running up the back of Mama's legs. She'd lift her right foot and rub the back of her left calf with it. Then the other. But always the right foot first.

(in Mama's voice) "Eases the aching, Eva."

That's what Mama told me about one thing or another my whole life. She had a cure for every ache known to womankind. Well, almost.

Carrying me home from the Sunnyside, she'd show me the moon.

(in Mama's voice) "Always where she should be, Eva! Like me, Eva. Like you!"

I wish I could remember what she told me the nights there was no moon.

Might have left me a little room to forgive.

We lived, just the two of us, in two rooms, two flights above the drugstore.

I remember going into the drugstore with Mama. Mr. Jordan Fennel owned it. Like his father and his father's father. Always thought people put too much store—no pun—in that kind of thing. Not everything that gets passed down is good.

Mr. Jordan Fennel gave us our rooms when he sold the store. No one to pass it on to.

Mr. Jordan Fennel always gave me a striped candy stick when Mama brought him his clothes. She mended and cleaned them every week. His wife was dead or crippled or something.

Mr. Jordan Fennel looked at Mama like a broody hen eyeing another's eggs.

That's how Mama described married men who ogle. She never seemed to notice when she was getting the once-over.

She was lonely.

(in Mama's voice) "Got so lonely sometimes, Eva, I'd hold my own hand at the bottom of the dishpan and talk dirty!"

Mama never seemed to consider any living man a solution. Waiting for something special, I guess.

I must have had a father, but if you listen to Mama, she did it all herself. Only thing she ever said was that he didn't like her soup!

I have so many questions. Is he dead? Did he come to Canada with us? Did we lose him on the way? Did Mama love him? Did *he* love *me*?

I could never do that to a child. What Mama did. Keeping it all for herself.

I used to make believe that Mr. Jordan Fennel was my father. He's dead now. Mama's dead and the drugstore has been a laundromat for a long time. And it's just me, living my life over the Duds & Suds.

It's convenient and I don't really mind the smells of other people's lives. When they're clean.

It's a different smell from mine. Lived in.

Not so much waiting.

What is it with waiting, anyway? It's not like it's some great virtue. Or some great accomplishment. You just wait.

It's easier than taking a chance.

Mama always said, *(in Mama's voice)* *"Wait, Eva, wait...things could change, Eva."*

No, Mama. You have to want to change things. Get out from under the comfort.

Most of the time I don't know what I'm waiting for. And don't recognise it when it arrives.

Like a flash of pink. Shocking. It disappears. Comes around again. And again.

It was a Sunday evening in the Duds & Suds. Mama did laundry Sunday night. Like it was written in the scripture. Thou shalt do thy laundry of a Sunday!

I'm nothing if I'm not Mama's daughter.

These days I sit in the laundromat on one of those hard plastic chairs and try to read.

Usually a book as drab as my laundry. Drab as my life.

Pink out of the corner of my eye. I will not look at it dead on. Mama says *(in Mama's voice)* *"If you do that, then the thing you're looking at slips away."*

I don't know what it is or how it made its way into my laundry, but I already know I don't want it to disappear.

Years back, I used to leave my clothes and trudge up the thirty-seven stairs, watch the café from Mama's favourite chair. Someone stole my clothes. My only dress, two pairs of slacks, one black, one brown, each with a matching twin set. My whole wardrobe.

Well, they left the uniforms. But took my underwear. I can't imagine anyone wanting it.

(in Mama's voice) *"Eva, don't use your underwear to get closer to God!"*

I get it now. Holey.

My eyes kept drifting to the dryer — brown black drab drab brown drab black. They could have been the exact clothes stolen twenty-five years earlier. What I was thinking was: Yup, that's about as much as has changed in my life!

I watched the clothes tumble to a stop, that split second of hesitation before they fall, one after the other, burying that sliver of pink.

What if I opened the door and it was gone? I plugged in more dimes. Kept the dryer going until the old guy came to lock up. Nearly fried my uniforms!

I didn't have time to fold anything. Just threw it all in my basket: Seventeen shades of nowhere and one lonely as I am pink sock. A child's. Not as big as the palm of my hand.

Usually, when someone misses a sock or a dishcloth, you tack it to the board. Most people here are regulars, so it's never long before things get claimed.

I didn't do that. I carried my laundry up up up with that pink sock on top. The crowning jewel. A prayer.

Didn't even count my way.

Me — who never puts one foot in front of the other without counting.

Me, who knows exactly how many steps from here to anywhere I've ever been.

A whole lot of going nowhere in short numbered steps.

Been counting my way since I was fifteen. You won't get pregnant if you get up and walk around is what he told me. He drove off, his taillights winking through the trees, and I kept walking, one two three — 11,827 steps to get back to the Sunnyside.

Evening is my favourite time here. Especially in winter. Day closing down at the same time as the café. Everyone gone home but me. I can slow down. Take my time.

Saturday nights I get to stay later than usual. The once-a-week jobs added to the daily jobs and I hardly have any home time to fill.

I remember nights I'd be in such a big hurry to play that jukebox and get to the dancing, I'd leave tables with no shakers, double up on others. Even leave some shakers empty.

Morning would show me quick enough what was needed to put things right.

I don't like morning.

I don't like kissing. I thought I would. I tried. His name was Rick. At least that's what it said on the sleeve of his jacket. He came in early morning. Working construction on the other side of Melbourne Street.

He was way too pretty. I flirted. I dared to dream getting away from Mama. Maybe being a hairdresser.

Took me two weeks to get that kiss. Front seat of his Chevy Malibu. Emptied me out and filled me up at the same time. One kiss.

I remember my bare feet jammed against the driver's-side window like two dead cod and while he was getting everything he wanted I picked the word Malibu off the glove box. It was just hanging there.

All I got, besides pregnant. A bun in the oven and the baker long gone.

I still have that word. Malibu.

It was a banner year for me. First and only kiss. Pregnant. First and only friend—Beth Ann.

I met Beth Ann in the park. We were both riding the merry-go-round. I liked to ride the black and white horse. I imagine he strains against the bit, fighting to be free. Each time around tossing his head, missing his chance. It's in his eyes.

Beth Ann likes the seat. She smiles and waves like a grand lady in a fine carriage!

Beth Ann Strickland was one of those stubbornly cheery people. You either love them or you want to smash their face in. Or both!

For a while, Beth Ann and I met in the park every Sunday afternoon.

I don't like Sunday.

Sunnyside's closed all day. I'm not really supposed to come over. But the Sunnyside is more home than work. Days off undo me. Like storm days when I was a child. My careful habit blown apart. A whole day of uncharted moments.

Sunday, the Sunnyside is a different place. Most everyone knows we're closed. Occasionally, someone tries the door or cups their hands between their face and the glass to peer inside. If they catch sight of me, the regulars see me as part and parcel. Strangers hardly see me at all. If they do, I just shake my head, point to the CLOSED sign and they're gone.

Peg tried the door once. Right around the time Mama died. Must be close to twenty years ago.

One minute there was nothing but my reflection, the black night behind it, and the next, the oval of Peg's face against the glass. Mama all over again. And me frozen.

Not breathing any more than was absolutely needed.

I'd lost track of her. And it weighed on me.

Finding that pink sock lightened me. Let me believe I could have Peg again. At the same time, it was so heavy I couldn't lift my foot to take the next step.

I'm here tonight, everything closed around me, waiting for Peg.

Tomorrow is my first Saturday off since Peg was born.

Thirty-six years and not one Saturday. Thirty-six years waiting on and waiting for. Never saw my part in it. Never understood the weight of it. The weight of waiting. See, Mama, I do have a sense of humour.

I hated Mama for making me such a fine waitress.

Mama washed dishes here for nearly thirty years. She wanted something better for me. Waitress extraordinaire! I've been waiting tables since I was sixteen.

I have never gone anywhere. Never been on a bus. Never rode a train. Never got farther than where my feet could take me. Only ever been in one car.

That's why I named my daughter Peg. Not short for Margaret. Just Peg. After the winged horse.

I didn't want this for Peg.

"Coffee hot enough? That cream's not off, is it? How do you want those eggs?"

Even when I was thinking "Why is there always an asshole?" it came out "Have a great day!"

All those years, waking every morning, believing, "Today something is going to happen!"

I almost made something happen once. Thought I was ready to try again.

He always sat right here.

He was whole-wheat toast, eggs over easy, corn relish with his hash browns, coffee black, and his smile opened doors in my skin.

Early morning, Monday to Friday, I could feel him walking long before he crossed Melbourne Street. I'd watch him all the way to the door. Just stop whatever I was doing and stare. What is it about anticipation that makes the reality so sickly?

He had a way of reading his paper that let me know it was okay to talk. Like he was always happy to put aside what he was doing for me.

Mama never liked him. *(in Mama's voice)* *"Too charming."* A grown-up version of Mr. Chevy Malibu.

(in Mama's voice) "What's a man like that want with a girl like you, Eva? One thing!"

I should have taken a Saturday off for him!

I went so far as to agree to him picking me up after work. And he came, knocking, pressing his face against the glass.

I watched the snow gather on his shoulders but I never moved. Eventually he went away. Wait long enough, everything goes away.

I sometimes dream him in the doorway, an empty cup in his long, fine fingers. I try to tell him I have nothing to give, but he whispers, "*You have everything I need.*" I step again and again into the possibility of him, but his tongue in my mouth is like Mama said, forked.

I swear by all the soup Mama made, I'm taking tomorrow off.

That's why I'm here doing Saturday things on a Friday.

Peg's coming. Here. Tonight.

> *Eva notices a rip in her uniform. She fingers it.*

Seems I'm coming apart at the seams!

Mama would have fixed this while I was on my feet, waiting tables. If I'd let her.

A one-woman wonder! She sewed my clothes, made my lunches out of what she called *(in Mama's voice) "good folks' leavings."*

Mama was always making something. Mostly it was to get some time for herself. I was never allowed to interrupt when Mama was working. So it was like she was all alone. She was happy then.

I'd be ready to burst and just when I thought I couldn't stay quiet for one more second, she'd set aside whatever she was working on and say,

(in Mama's voice) "Talk, Eva, talk."

I still have the box Mama made me from a box that Mr. Jordan Fennel gave her. It held four bars of soap.

Took Mama forever to use it up, but once she did, she covered the box with material from a rag of a dress not even Mama could save. She lined it with a bit of an old silk slip.

Sometimes when I open the box I think I can still smell that blue iris soap. But of course that's just foolishness. I keep everything that means something to me in it.

It's not a big box.

Peg will have it when I'm dead.

Mama did everything for me. She saw me off to school, taught me how to cross the street. Showed me how to wear my clothes as if I had a closet full.

Mama believed that what you're wearing when you die is what you wear for eternity. No matter how they gussie up the body. And she believed whatever you've done most of in your life, you just keep on with.

If that's true, Mama's making soup in a yellow apron with the tiniest blue flowers. She lived making soup.

Soup every night from bones the butcher saved for a dog we didn't own.

(in Mama's voice) "Soup to build a life on, Eva."

Split pea ham, beef barley, pork potato. Chicken not so often. People bought that with the bone in.

Mama could have had a whole chicken. And the butcher too. Some of the scraps he saved her said a whole lot more than soup.

Mama was a charmer. She had an innocent, flirty way about her. And she used it. The butcher, the baker, the candlestick maker — she had them all on a wire. She'd pluck it just as much as was needed to get whatever she thought I had to have. Always me. Never what she might have needed. Wanted.

Mama believed it was soup Peg needed. Soup that would bring her home. Batch after batch and Mama sure that each one would be THE one that Peg would smell from Wichita or Cheyenne or wherever she was and realise she couldn't live one more day without us.

I wonder what exactly Beth Ann told Peg about us. Mama and me.

About the time Peg was five, Mama started setting a place for her.

(in Mama's voice) "Old enough to be eating late with us, Eva!"

I washed Peg's dishes, carried them to the cupboard night after night, though she never once used them.

Can't devote yourself to one person like Mama did. Trying to give them what they want before they know they want it.

Some wanting is easy to name. New drapes. A slow cooker. A walk in the park. Some wanting we can't ever name.

Funny how the regulars here are like family and I get into the routine of what they want and just go about doing it. Comfortable.

New customers worry me.

I remember a Saturday morning. Busiest time of the week. The other waitress didn't show. Just me and Frank. He was still alive, so I know I was pretty young.

I don't remember people's names. I do remember what they eat. What they want from me. She only came in that one time, travelling through, or didn't like the food. Doesn't matter. Eggs Benedict, seven-grain toast — no butter — and the strongest black coffee we could offer. That's what she said. "Give me the strongest black coffee you can offer."

She didn't speak again until she'd eaten, paid up, pressing a twenty dollar tip on me. Felt sorry, I guess. One little waitress and a café full of hungry people.

She held on to my arm until I had no choice but to look her in the eye. It frightened me that someone could see that far.

"What's your name?"

I reached for my breast pocket—where my nametag should be. Frank wasn't going to be happy if I lost another. It was there.

Eva.

"Well, Eva. You watch yourself. Or you're going to wake up one morning and realise you have everything you need, everything you want, and it's not enough."

Now there's a tip I can live without!

Nothing — no thing is ever going to be enough until we allow what we truly want. Some things take up all your wanting room. Like wanting to fill your daughter's bowl, once and once again. And there it is. Said out loud, walking towards you, hand in hand with the possibility that it might be enough.

I was Mama's out-loud wanting. She made a place for me, gave me everything.

I gave my daughter away.

Like a fucking puppy.

I couldn't bear to touch her.

Do you want to hold your baby, Eva?

Noooooooooooooooooooooo!

Mama made me.

The baby cried all the time, except when Mama was there, holding her. I could see Mama's plan. How she'd use us. An excuse for her own little life.

(in Mama's voice) "Eva, you can't fill your life up with someone else's living."

But isn't that what you're doing, Mama? Only time she ever slapped me.

I understood then. I'd never get away. We'd never get away.

I kept Peg for five days.

It wasn't as heartless as it sounds. Not like I handed her over to the first person who walked by. I gave her to my friend. Beth Ann.

Beth Ann wore an overcoat of cheery. She kept it closed up tight but sometimes I'd catch a glimpse of what ran underneath. Such a sadness. Turns out it all had to do with not being able to carry a baby full term. We met a lot of times, had a lot of talks before I found that out.

We all have our sad stories. I don't want to hear them. It's that foot in the door thing. I can't let that happen.

Some stories you hear even when you're working hard not to.

He ordered dry toast every morning for a week. Never once ate more than a bite. And hot milk.

After the first morning, he timed his arrival so most of the regulars were cleared out. He liked to talk and because I was the only waitress not rushing out back for a smoke, I was the one got talked to.

I was busy pretending he was my father coming to find me, waiting for the right moment to call me daughter!

So most of what he said I didn't hear.

I asked him on his last morning what brought him here.

His brother.

I thought that was all he was going to say.

Then he told me. When he was eight, his brother five, they got taken up by different families. Separated for seventy years. His brother lived right here in this town for all of those years and Mr. Hot Milk, Dry Toast lived out west.

Then someone found someone and it was all arranged. Planned out to the second-to-last detail. Second-to-last, because they sure hadn't planned the last — his brother getting killed by a car the day before he arrived.

That first day in the café was his brother's funeral. *So why are you still here*? I asked him. He didn't think he could change his ticket.

Three whole days on the bus he said. "We could have had those days if I'd hopped a plane." Time wasted he said.

Try wasting a lifetime. I could have had all these years with Peg.

I was sixteen and so sure I knew. My decision was white. Blistering white. Like salt.

(in Mama's voice) "Titch to teaspoon, Eva, salt makes the soup!"

Salt of the earth. Salt in the wound. It leached out every bit of colour. Except for that pink sock and the startled blue of Peg's eyes.

Beth Ann came to see the baby and to say goodbye. They were moving. Her husband had a new job. They'd start over.

No, they wouldn't try again for a baby.

I told her we should meet in the park the next day. One last get-together.

I packed up everything Mama had sewn for Peg, and while Mama washed dishes across the street, I walked the four blocks over to that park on the corner of Main and Pleasant, kissed Beth Ann on the cheek, and gave her the baby.

My baby.

We didn't stay friends. You can't.

Beth Ann tried. Wrote to me. Fat envelopes that had to have pictures in them.

I didn't open Beth Ann's letters.

I might have kept them, except for Mama. It scared me the way she never stopped looking for Peg. Never stopped peering into carriages, playgrounds, other people's lives.

She must have taken a billion steps, searching.

More steps than my whole life.

I did see Beth Ann once. Shopping. Just before Christmas the year Peg turned four. I went to the mall. There was Beth Ann, her cart overflowing. Pink. Pink. And more pink. Toys and frills.

She rattled on. They'd moved again. She worked part-time now. Had another baby girl.

Not another. Peg is mine. My baby. Not another.

> *Beat.*

She won't say Peg and I can't. Like Peg is a bullet to the brain.

They don't call her Peg. Margaret. A dead, dowdy, porridge kind of name. Until Beth Ann says it out loud.

It's all I can hear—a wrap-around, a hold-you-close-forever song, an anthem, a prayer answered in a word. Margaret.

Thinking I didn't love Peg was like trying to swallow a fishbone.

All the frilly little outfits are pulsing, rising up — a gaudy, headless merry-go-round circling me. I turn away.

One, two, three. She called my name at fifteen. I didn't slow but I heard. "Eva. Eva! God damn it, Eva, she's happy."

Not me! Not me! I screamed at every passerby. I forgot to count.

Halfway home I knew I was lost. More lost than I'd ever been.

> *Beat.*

The minute Peg was born, the minute she got that first whiff of the world, you could tell she figured she'd made a mistake.

Why did it take me so long?

I handed her over and there was nothing. Not one bit of relief. Just a hole. A 7 lb 5 oz hole. I filled my head with numbers so I couldn't feel.

So I wouldn't have to know that all I'd done was trade one fear for another. The fear of never getting away from Mama for the fear of never having Peg. Walking away from Peg...my whole body ached with the weight of her gone.

Walking away takes more steps than walking to.

But I already knew that. I'd been counting my way to the park and home again ever since I knew I was pregnant.

So that day, giving Peg to Beth Ann, I should have been 5,321 steps from home.

When I'd taken every one of the steps. I could see the drugstore, the light in our window. I could smell Mama's soup. But I wasn't home.

I could see my life from then on: how I'd pull each day from the one before and that from the one before. Thirty-seven steps down to the street. Fifty-two to cross. Each day kept wooden and falsely bright, achingly the same. But smaller.

Right there, not a hundred steps from the Sunnyside, I had nothing left. I thought I might borrow some steps from tomorrow. But I couldn't start that. God knows where I'd end. So I stood there until way past midnight. Mama came to get me. Her face wild!

(in Mama's voice) *"What have you done, Eva? What have you done to me?"*

I killed us, Mama.

Beat.

I don't like time on my own.

While Mama was living I took a week off every spring. Cleaned our apartment top to bottom. Well, not her room. Not the room Jordan Fennel cleared out for her. Meant we each had a space of our own. I was not allowed in Mama's room. She kept it locked. The door was black with Storage written in red paint that flowed down like blood. It scared me a little. I might never have known what she was up to if I hadn't come home early one afternoon, sick as a dog.

I made my way to her room. Wanted her to know I was home and going to bed. Mama liked to know what was going on with me.

She had an old table in there and it was covered with tiny bits of wood, cloth. The room smelled of glue. She was building a dollhouse. So fine, so delicate.

There was a whole family. I mostly remember the father, standing outside the house, a briefcase tucked up under his arm. Coming home to the perfect life Mama built. She was hemming little curtains and talking away to Peg.

I never said a word. Just turned and went down to my room.

I do that a lot. Walk away, not saying a word.

What good would it have done to tell Mama that Peg was too old to play with dolls? Except maybe with her own children.

Peg has at least one. I read that in the only letter of Beth Ann's I opened. It came years after the others. I thought it had been long enough…

I was a grandmother. Technically.

Beat.

Mama and I knew just how lonely technically can be.

The day she finished the dollhouse, Mama dropped dead in the middle of Melbourne Street. I saw her from the Sunnyside, turning from our apartment to the café and back again.

The same three gestures over and over. Right hand in her pocket searching, left hand to shield her eyes from the sun, then both hands to her mouth. Stroke can do that. Creates a loop and you go round and round like a merry-go-round until you don't.

Five full circles before she dropped.

By the time the ambulance arrived, all of Melbourne Street smelled of Mama's soup.

She'd left a pot on the stove. No damage but smoke. Took years to get rid of the smell. Mama's chair still holds a little.

I even went to work on the day of her funeral. Didn't know anything else to do. Anywhere else to be.

Haven't taken any day but Sunday off since. And only Sunday, like I said, because we're closed. Until the new owner. Bud. A real stickler for the rules. Made me take this week off.

Two days to clean. Two days to sit in Mama's chair in my uniform. Praying all the other waitresses would come down sick, leave Bud desperate. I'd be ready!

This morning I walked to the park. The merry-go-round had been shut down. There was an "out of order" sign hanging off my favourite horse. The black and white.

The kids were playing 'Mother May I?'

Mama may I? Mama may I?

I stayed most of the day in the park and when I got home I went up to Mama's room. Last time I was in there was to pick out her burying dress. I took her locket then. It holds the only picture of Peg and me. I don't know which one of us looks more frightened.

I couldn't bury it with Mama.

Today I took the dollhouse, carried it down to my room, cleared the top of my bureau with a sweep of my arm.

I set it on the bureau, arranged the whole family in front of the house.

The baby was missing. It broke my heart. That one little sadness, that foot in the door…

I was so tired I thought I must be dying. So I put on a clean uniform and crawled into bed to wait.

I couldn't sleep.

   Beat.

I woke a couple of hours ago, put my shoes on, pleased that I was not going to spend eternity with everyone seeing my big toe out the hole in my pantyhose.

Then it came to me: Eva, you fool — thinking you're dying so you don't have to face living.

I am every bit as alive as I've ever been.

Peg will be here soon.

I'm going to do it this time. I'm going to hold my baby.

I'm going to tell her Peg is for Pegasus. Peg. My out-loud wanting.

I going to say I'm sorry.

I'm going to tell her about the box. She won't know how it smelled or how the purple taffeta was so dark it was almost black. Unless I tell her.

What would she make of what's inside? A photograph of a young man in uniform. He's been my father ever since I stole the picture from Mama's drawer. My eyes are his eyes.

But I don't know who he was, not really.

Mama's locket.

A child's pink sock.

And Malibu.

> *Eva repeats the next three gestures three times as she turns. She wipes her palms on her uniform, checks for her name tag, smooths her hair. Blackout.*

About the playwright

Pam Calabrese MacLean's writing for the stage includes *Her Father's Barn* (Atlantic Fringe Festival (NS) 2001; Festival Antigonish Late Night (NS) 2002; London Fringe (ON) 2005; Liverpool International Play Festival (NS) 2006; Uno Festival (BC) 2007; Mulgrave Theatre (NS) 2008; King's Theatre (NS) 2010), *Is it Wednesday?* (King's Shorts (NS) 2010; Six Women International Playwriting Festival Colourado (US) 2011; Theatre Antigonish (NS) 2012, and *Awake* (King's Shorts (NS) 2009; Theatre Antigonish (NS) 2012. MacLean is also the author of two poetry books and two children's books. She lives in Nova Scotia.

Interview

The seeds for *Sunnyside Café* were sown in 1971 as I rode the train to see my mother. The train was packed and I sat facing a woman and her twelve-year-old daughter. They were two of the most confident, self-assured women I had met in my twenty-one years of life. They remain so. The mother told me how her daughter was just a newborn when they came to Canada, fleeing someone or something; how she wrapped her baby tight and left her in the apartment while she worked; how the butcher saved them bones for a dog they didn't own. The seeds became a long poem in 2005 (CBC Radio) and morphed into *Sunnyside Café* by fall 2009.

I started to write for the stage to create strong parts for women, more mature women. Eva from *Sunnyside Café* is the youngest of my women, but originally her mother was to be more than a voice. I also wanted very much to explore adoption. I am adopted, as is my eldest son. Some would say it's hereditary!

I spent my whole life lying about my feelings for the woman who bore me. I remember my son once tearfully asked "Why didn't she [his mother] want me?" and I managed, with difficulty, to think how lucky I was that I didn't have that feeling of abandonment. It wasn't until I tried for several years to write a happy ending, a reconciliation, for *Sunnyside Café* and couldn't, that I had to acknowledge that I didn't think my birth mother deserved these things. Then the ending practically wrote itself.

I wanted to keep this story rooted in women. Women, whether they have birthed, adopted, lost, or denied a child, understand the weight of Eva's choice. I wanted to explore a mother-daughter relationship. Women become who they are because of, or in spite of, their mothers. Eva, in the end, empowers herself through her determination to make things change. It's just tragically late.

The title *Sunnyside Café* came from the meeting on the train. That is where the mother first worked in Canada.

Eco-Audit
Printing this book using Rolland Enviro 100 Book
instead of virgin fibres paper saved the following resources:

Trees	Solid Waste	Water	Air Emissions
2	107kg	7,046 L	277 kg